Praise for Meb Keflezighi and *Meb for Mortals*

"Meb Keflezighi is one of the most passionate and dedicated runners in the world. He is an icon for American distance runners. Now Meb has chosen to share his training secrets and tips with the world. Every runner, from the beginner to elite, can gain tremendous insight and wisdom in *Meb for Mortals*. Get ready to take your running to another level with help from Meb."
—**KARA GOUCHER, two-time Olympian**

"Since our days at UCLA, I have seen Meb work hard to get the best out of himself. The longevity of his career is simply amazing. *Meb for Mortals* gives unique insight into how Meb has been able to get better with age."
—**BARON DAVIS, two-time NBA All-Star**

"Having trained with Meb over the years, I know first-hand his love of running and his commitment to improvement. In *Meb for Mortals*, runners of all abilities and motivation levels will be inspired and able to develop with his sage advice."
—**DEENA KASTOR, American record holder in the marathon and half-marathon**

"My experiences as a competitive runner have had a direct impact on the way I operate in business. To become a success in business, sports or life, you must set challenging, personally meaningful goals and be accountable to those goals. In *Meb for Mortals*, Meb shows us all how he does this, and how you can, too."
—**JOHN LEGERE, President and CEO, T-Mobile US**

"I have admired Meb Keflezighi as a runner and as a person for many years, and seeing him win in Boston—my hometown—last year was deeply gratifying for me. If you want to achieve your distance running goals while maintaining a healthy balance of training and family life, *Meb for Mortals* is the book for you."
—**SHALANE FLANAGAN, Olympic bronze medalist and American record holder in the 10,000 meters**

"Meb is one of the greatest champions I've ever known in all of my many different lives. His kindness, gentleness, persistence, perseverance, and steely determination have, combined with his unique athletic prowess, helped him to achieve remarkable things both as a runner and as a human force of nature. Please, I challenge you to take just one step in Meb's shoes by reading his brilliant and inspiring new book, *Meb for Mortals*. You will never look at life, running—or anything else—the same way again."
—**BILL WALTON, Basketball Hall of Fame 1993**

Meb
FOR MORTALS

How to Run, Think, and Eat

like a Champion Marathoner

Meb Keflezighi

with Scott Douglas

RODALE.

To the running community.
You have given me so much
knowledge, great experiences,
and meaningful friendships.
—MK

Rodale books may be purchased for business or promotional use or for special sales. For information, please write to: Special Markets Department, Rodale Inc., 733 Third Avenue, New York, NY 10017.

Printed in the United States of America

Rodale Inc. makes every effort to use acid-free ⊛, recycled paper ♻.

Book design by Jeff Batzli
All photographs by Alex Aristei, except for the following pages: John Tlumacki/The Boston Globe/Getty Images, page viii; Jim Rogash/Stringer/Getty Images, page 66; CHIP EAST/Reuters/Corbis, page 81.
Meb for Mortals exercises were shot on location at Snowcreek Athletic Club, Mountain Lakes, California.

Library of Congress Cataloging-in-Publication Data is on file with the publisher.

ISBN-13: 978–1–62336–547–9 paperback

Distributed to the trade by Macmillan

2   4   6   8   10   9   7   5   3   1   paperback

We inspire and enable people to improve their lives and the world around them.
rodalebooks.com

CONTENTS

FOREWORD BY TONY DUNGY VI

INTRODUCTION BE LIKE MEB IX

Chapter 1 **Think like Meb**. 1

Chapter 2 **Run like Meb** 13

Chapter 3 **Train like Meb** 41

Chapter 4 **Race like Meb** 67

Chapter 5 **Eat like Meb**. 85

Chapter 6 **Strengthen like Meb**. 97

Chapter 7 **Stretch like Meb** 135

Chapter 8 **Cross-Train like Meb** 165

Chapter 9 **Recover like Meb** 177

ACKNOWLEDGMENTS 189

ABOUT THE AUTHORS 191

INDEX 192

FOREWORD

IN 2004, I was beginning my third season as head coach of the Indianapolis Colts. On August 29, I was in my office at the Colts training facility, working on the game plan for our final preseason game. I had the television on, trying to keep an eye on the Summer Olympics, which were going on in Athens, Greece. The Olympic Marathon was being run that day, and as the race unfolded, it became apparent that an American, Meb Keflezighi, was going to have a chance to win a medal. In the final miles of the race, three men broke away from the pack and staged a grueling charge to the finish line in the quest for gold. Meb ran his best time of the season to finish in second place and become the first American to win a medal in the Marathon in 28 years. I didn't know him at the time, but I remember being so proud that an American man had done so well in the signature event of Olympic track and field.

Little did I know that I would one day get to meet Meb Keflezighi. Five years later, in 2009, I was retired from coaching and working for NBC's *Football Night in America*. Our Sunday evening broadcasts were done from Rockefeller Center in New York City, and my normal routine on Sunday mornings was to take a walk through Central Park before heading into the studio. On this November morning my walk was disrupted because the park was blocked off to accommodate the runners in the New York City Marathon. And who would win that day but Meb. At the age of 34, he would run his personal best time and become the first American man to win the race in 27 years.

Shortly afterward we got a chance to meet, and I found out that we had a few things in common, including our love of competition and our Christian faith. I had been blessed to win the biggest prize in football when our Colts team won Super Bowl XLI in 2007, but along the way I'd had some disappointments. I always felt it was my faith in God that allowed me to keep chasing after my goals, and I found out that the same is true of Meb. But, as I got to know him, I came to see that some of the disappointments I had experienced were nothing compared to what he had gone through.

As I learned about his life story, I was blown away. Meb was born in Eritrea, one of ten children. He and his family were refugees who came to the United States in 1987. Distance running became his love and he enjoyed tremendous success, but he had to overcome several injuries along the way. He'd actually had treatment in Tampa performed by one of our Buccaneers' team doctors after a particularly severe injury. There was no guarantee that he would ever be able to run at such a high level again.

Through all the injuries and disappointments, however, he never gave in to discouragement. He always felt the Lord had other things for him to accomplish, so he continued to set goals for himself. In 2013 there was a tragic bombing at the Boston Marathon, which resulted in 5 deaths and injuries to almost 300 people. When that happened, Meb told himself he wanted to win the Boston Marathon as a tribute to those people. As noble as that goal was, it just didn't seem possible. It had been almost 30 years since an American had won this race. But the next year, just two weeks shy of his 39th birthday, Meb won the Boston Marathon. That made him the first person ever to win the Boston Marathon, the New York City Marathon, and an Olympic medal in the Marathon.

How did he do it? In *Meb for Mortals,* he shares his secrets. Actually, they're not secrets but merely the things that he has learned throughout his career in running. In detailing his steps of setting goals, working hard, and persevering no matter what obstacles may come in his path, Meb gives his formula for success in running and in life. This book will give you instructions on running and training that will help you whether you're a casual runner or pursuing an Olympic medal of your own.

I believe you'll love this book because in addition to telling you *what* to do, it tells you *how* to do it. Not only does Meb talk about the physical aspects of training, but he also takes a look at mental preparation. How do you prepare yourself to succeed? How can you stay on course when the going gets tough? How do you make sure you stay focused on the little details that separate the winners from the also-rans?

If you enjoy running, I know you're going to enjoy this book. So dig in and get some tips from arguably the greatest distance runner in United States history.

Tony Dungy
Former Super Bowl–winning head coach and
New York Times bestselling author

INTRODUCTION

Be like Meb

MY MULTIFACETED PROGRAM FOR RUNNING SUCCESS

"How did you do it?"

That's a question I heard again and again after I won the 2014 Boston Marathon. How had I beaten the strongest field in Boston Marathon history to become the first American man to win the race since 1983? How did someone with the 15th-fastest personal best in the field come out on top? How had I rebounded from the worst marathon of my life only 5 months earlier? How did a guy who had won an Olympic medal 10 years before and had suffered many injuries in the decade since run a personal best just 2 weeks before his 39th birthday?

The week after my victory, *Runner's World* published an article about my training before Boston. The response to the article was gratifying. So many people said they were inspired by my Boston win and how I'd prepared for it. They found that my approach made a lot of sense, and they wanted to know how to implement it in their own running.

So I wrote this book. It describes in unprecedented detail how I prepare to take on the best runners in the world. More important, it shows everyday runners how to put into practice the training, nutritional, and mental principles that have guided me throughout my long career, which in addition to my Boston win includes that 2004 Olympic silver medal and the 2009 New York City Marathon title.

Meb for Mortals isn't just for hard-core competitors. I wrote this book for all runners eager to learn how to most effectively improve and enjoy their running. For some, that might mean learning how to train for a 5-K or a marathon. For others, it might mean getting practical advice on how to eat for health and performance while also keeping their weight under control. For yet others, it might mean guidance on what exercises will best help them avoid injury and improve their running form. With the great range of topics covered in *Meb for Mortals*, my goal is tell you what I do and why I do it that way and to show you how to apply my example to your situation.

What's in This Book

I'M NOT the most talented guy. Whatever I've achieved stems from how I apply the three keys to success in running (and life): good goals, commitment, and hard work. Those factors determine everything I do, from which races I run to my tactics in those races, from how far my long runs are to what stretches I do, and from how I deal with aging to, believe it or not, watching my weight.

You might scoff at a champion marathoner saying he's not all that talented. Obviously, I have pretty good natural running ability. In 7th grade, without any formal training, I ran a 5:20 mile in phys ed class. That's an excellent time for someone of that age but certainly not unprecedented. To compete as well as I do, I've always had to do more than just run. Since high school, when I first got serious about running, I've supplemented my basic running workouts with stretching, strengthening, form drills, and other practices designed to help me get the most out of my training. On top of that, I have to make difficult choices about how to spend my time. For example, in high school I gave up soccer, which I'd played while growing up and had wanted to be a professional at, to focus on running.

Since becoming a professional runner in 1998, I've had a reputation as a methodical trainer. People say, "Meb has been so good for so long because he does all the little things." It's true that I'm dedicated to eating well, recovering well, working on my running form, cross-training, and staying strong and flexible. But it's important to realize that I don't consider those "little things." They're integral to being the best runner I can be; when done day in and day out, they're like compound interest, building to something big over time.

Let me give you an illustration. One of my guiding philosophies is "prehab, not rehab." By that I mean it's better to spend a little time daily working to build your running body than to spend a lot of time doing the same exercises because you're injured. Strengthening, stretching, form drills, cross-training, and recovery practices are among the ways I implement the "prehab, not rehab" principle. Without being diligent about those matters, I wouldn't be able to train as hard, and I would get injured more often. That would mean I wouldn't have won an Olympic medal in 2004 or the New York City Marathon 5 years later. And there's no way I would have won the Boston Marathon 5 years after that if I just ran. So, to me, they're hardly "little things."

Everything you do in your running life is interrelated. So while you'll find *Meb for Mortals* organized by distinct topics—training, racing, diet, etc.—you'll also find references within each chapter to the topics of other chapters. How you recover (Chapter 9) affects how you do your long runs (Chapter 3). What you eat (Chapter 5) affects whether you meet your goals (Chapter 1). How good your running form is (Chapter 2) contributes to how well you race (Chapter 4). And so on.

I also devote a good part of this book to the "little things," because I think they're a neglected part of most runners' programs. You might think, "I barely have time to get in my runs, let alone stretch and strengthen and do form drills and all that other stuff." But I'm not asking for hours of your time. In the relevant chapters, I'll show you exactly what I do in terms of things like stretching and strengthening, and then suggest how to easily incorporate these exercises into your own schedule for maximum gain. Taking 10 minutes a day to become a faster, more efficient, and more injury-resistant runner sounds like a pretty good investment to me.

My Love of Running

IF YOU'RE like me, you appreciate how running improves your life. You like how you feel while you're running and after a run. You like being healthier and more in control of your destiny. You like the camaraderie and the time alone. You like being outside enjoying nature. You like pushing yourself and the satisfaction that comes from working toward a goal. You like how clear-cut it is, how you get out of it what you put into it. You like that you get to do it on your terms, as casually or seriously as you want. You simply like telling yourself, "I'm a runner."

I intend to be a runner long after I stop trying to win the biggest marathons in the world. By now it's in my blood. I love to sweat—when I sweat I feel like I've accomplished something. I love reflecting on what I've done and on how it will help me in the future. And in that afterglow, I'm motivated to do other positive things for my long-term health. I want to stretch. I want to do my core workout. I want to eat well. A whole healthy lifestyle springs from just getting out the door. Going for even a short run makes me appreciate how fortunate I am to be able to do this amazing activity and have fun while I'm doing it.

Almost all runners want to stay in the sport as long as possible. I hope *Meb for Mortals* helps you do that. As I joked after winning Boston, my career goals have now been 100 percent fulfilled, so I'm happy to divulge the secrets of my success. If you're ready to get the best out of yourself, let's start exploring how my principles and practices can take your running to new levels.

Think like Meb

How the right mind-set leads to running success

IN THE INTRODUCTION, I said that three key things that determine your long-term success as a runner are good goals, commitment, and hard work.

Only one of those items is physical. The other two are psychological. That's how important I think the mental side of running is. And that's why I'm putting this chapter before those on different types of hard workouts and what to eat and how to strengthen and stretch. If you've defined what you want to achieve, then the running part is easy. With the right goals and the commitment to keep pursuing them, you can achieve more in running than you ever thought possible.

Why Goals Are Important

GOALS FORM your road map to success. You won't get near your potential without having good goals. That's true in running just like it is in other areas, such as work and finances. I think we're wired as humans to dream of what might be and then figure out how to make that dream a reality.

I never would have won the Boston and New York City Marathons, plus an Olympic silver medal, without setting the goals to do so. I might have occasionally run a good race if setting goals wasn't a key part of my approach, but I wouldn't have been able to regularly beat some of the best runners in the world. Everything that I've achieved physically in running started psychologically, with the simple thought, "I want to do this."

Running is especially well suited to goal setting, because your progress can so easily be quantified and tracked. Running is also well suited to goal setting because, let's face it, it's not the world's easiest sport. Goals help you maintain the consistency that's so important to succeeding as a runner. Goals also help you experience the special joy that comes from not giving in, from pushing through discomfort to accomplish something that's meaningful to you.

You might say that you don't want to be like that with your running—you just want to run to relieve stress, not create more of it, and that the rest of your life is plenty goal oriented.

I'm fine with that approach. But you might not realize that you probably already set goals in your running. You don't head out the door saying, "I'm going to run until I get tired." You have a route in mind or a general idea of the duration your run will be. You probably also usually run a certain number of times each week, and you probably aren't happy if something keeps you from getting in that many. So you already have some basic running goals, even if you've never stated them as goals. It might be the case that setting more-formal goals will help you enjoy your running even more.

Running goals don't have to be competitive goals. I have a friend who is a dedicated runner who asks me, "Why would I want to pay to enter a race? I run fast or slow at my own leisure." There's nothing wrong with that approach. Running can accommodate all sorts of goals—running a certain number of times a week, running enough to maintain a good weight, finishing a half-marathon without walking, and so on. Whatever motivates you to regularly get out the door gets my stamp of approval.

Qualities of a Good Goal

THE BEST goals have certain elements that make your success more likely. Here's what I think good goals have in common.

A GOOD GOAL HAS PERSONAL MEANING. Nobody ever told me, "You have to win the 2014 Boston Marathon" or "You have to make the 2012 Olympic team." Those were goals I set for myself. When I told myself, "I want to win Boston," it just felt right. I knew that chasing that goal would motivate me to do what was necessary to achieve it and that doing so would require me to do my best.

Your goals should have that same pull on you. They should be things you want to achieve for yourself, not to meet someone else's expectations. Training to reach a goal requires a lot of hard work. When you hit a tough stretch, either physically or mentally, if the goal you're working toward has deep significance for you, you'll find a way to persevere. But if someone else thrust the goal upon you, when you hit tough stretches, you're going to think, "Wait, why am I doing this?"

Most of us have enough areas in our lives where we have to meet others' expectations. Let your running be about your own hopes and dreams.

A GOOD GOAL IS SPECIFIC. Notice how specific the goals I set for myself were: I wanted to win the 2014 Boston Marathon. I wanted to make the 2012 Olympic team. There's no ambiguity there. I knew exactly what I wanted to do, and that helped me decide how I should go about doing it.

Here's a time example. At the beginning of 2001, one of my goals for the year was to break the American record for 10,000 meters. The time I needed to beat was 27:20.56. It doesn't get much more specific than knowing to the 100th of a second what I needed to run to meet my goal. That specificity told me exactly what pace I needed to run in the race and what times to hit in workouts. Thanks to the guidance provided by my specific goal, I was able to run 27:13.98 that year, an American record that stood until 2010.

Now consider if I had stated my goals more generally: I want to run well at Boston. I want to run faster in the 10,000 meters. "Run well" is so much more subjective than "win." How would I know during and after the race if I'd run well? And how would I know what to do in training to meet that goal? Saying simply that I wanted to improve my 10-K personal best is more specific than the Boston example, but it still wouldn't have been as motivating. My personal best when I set the goal was 27:53.63. I was a young professional runner and improving rapidly. I could have run 27:53.62 and met the goal of improving my personal best. While you should celebrate every personal best, at that stage in my career I wanted to aim higher.

So include an element of specificity: "I want to run 30 seconds faster for 5-K" instead of "I want to run faster," or "I want to run 5 days a week" instead of "I want to run more."

A GOOD GOAL IS CHALLENGING BUT REALISTIC. Your goals should require you to reach outside your comfort zone while remaining within the realm of possibility. If you've run a 2:05 half-marathon, then making your next goal to run a 2:05 half-marathon won't be all that compelling. You've already done it, so how motivating will it be to do it again?

But you shouldn't go to the other extreme and say, "I want to lower my half-marathon best from 2:05 to 1:30." Your goal should be attainable within a reasonable time frame. (More on that below.) You might eventually get down to 1:30, but it's most likely going to occur in stages: from

2:05 to 1:58, then 1:48, then 1:43, and so on. Long-distance running is not the sport for people who crave instant gratification.

Making a Boston victory my goal was realistic. In my case, I had finished third and fifth in previous Boston marathons, so winning the race wasn't outside the realm of possibility. Trying to win certainly required reaching, given that the race was held 2 weeks before my 39th birthday and I had the 15th-fastest personal best in the field.

An example of a too-ambitious goal for me would be saying, "I want to break the

DON'T GET COCKY!

WHILE YOU WANT to be ambitious in setting goals, you should also include an element of caution.

Think about when you started driving. If you were like me, you were so careful. But over time most of us think, "I got this. Driving is second nature." It's when we let down our guard that accidents happen.

The same is true with running. Once you get fit and things start going well, it's natural to think, "I got this running thing down." You might be tempted to go crazy with your goals, such as suddenly going from 20 miles a week to 40 miles or doing twice as many hard runs a week. For a while you might get away with it. But if you let down your guard for too long and ignore the fact that making gradual progress is the best way to meet your long-term goals, you'll pay the price. Just as another car can seem to come out of nowhere when you glance at your phone while you're driving, an injury can "suddenly" pop up when you overreach in your running goals.

world record." I've almost always raced for position, running whatever time is necessary to place as high as possible. But some of the major marathons are set up more like track races on the road, with pacemakers to take the top contenders through 30 kilometers at world-record pace. If I made breaking the world record my goal, that would mean taking more than 5½ minutes off my personal best in one race. That's unlikely at this stage in my career. A more realistic but still challenging marathon time goal for me would be to lower my best from 2:08:37 to 2:07:30 and move into third on the all-time US list.

Part of realistic goal setting is using your knowledge of running and of yourself to define the range of possible results. Before my first Olympic final, the 10,000-meter race at the 2000 Sydney Olympics, my father told me, "You're going to win tonight." I said, "Wait a minute! Dad, I'm not going to win." He said, "You cannot think negatively. Don't say that. You're going to win tonight." I explained to him that I hadn't yet broken 28:00, while the two top contenders, Haile Gebrselassie and Paul Tergat, had run faster than 26:30. I said, "Dad, I can't beat them tonight. But I hope to beat them someday." My father was disappointed, but I was being realistic. And in the next Olympics, I won the silver medal in the Olympic Marathon while Tergat, then the world-record holder, finished 10th.

A GOOD GOAL HAS A TIME ELEMENT. It's human nature to be motivated by a

GOAL ACCOUNTABILITY

I WRITE DOWN my goals so there's no question of what I'm aiming for. There it is in black and white: "I want to do this, I want to do that." If you're like me, you'll find that regularly seeing your goals is a way to keep yourself honest.

I also write down long-term goals, such as where I want to be in 5 or 10 years. It can be fun, or at least interesting, to look back on those long-term goals. Sometimes I've seen an old list and thought, "Hey, I've done four out of five. I feel good about that." Other times it's been more like, "One out of four. Well, that's better than none. Better keep working hard."

deadline. Having a date by which you want to reach your goal helps you plan how to reach it ("My marathon is in 14 weeks, so I need to come up with a training program to get from today to race day") and provides urgency ("My marathon is in 14 weeks, so I better get training!"). When I was training for the 2014 Boston Marathon, I told my wife, Yordanos, that it was my last chance to win the race. If, at that stage of my career, I'd said, "I'd like to win the Boston Marathon someday," it never would have happened.

There's a sweet spot for how far away your goal should be. If you say, "I want to run this year's New York City Marathon," and the race is in 2 weeks and you've been running twice a week, well, good luck. But if you say, "I want to run the 2025 New York City Marathon," that's so distant that it's unlikely to motivate you to work toward it.

For most runners, 3 to 6 months is a good range for achieving a main goal. That's enough time to do the work to achieve it but also close enough to remain motivating on a daily basis. I also recommend (and set) yearly goals and even 5-year goals, but in the context of what I've been describing, this range of a few to several months works well for most runners.

To work toward that goal, set shorter-term goals. Decide where you should be at the end of each month leading up to your goal, and then break those months into week-by-week progress toward that month-end goal. For example, say you're currently running twice a week, and your goal is to comfortably run 5 days a week 3 months from now. You'd then say that after the 1st month, you want to be at 3 days a week. In that 1st month, you'd have some weeks with two runs and some with three, gradually making your way to 3 days a week being your new norm. Then in the 2nd month you'd do the same thing to be comfortable running 4 days a week, and repeat the process in the 3rd month to get to 5 days a week.

Every week, evaluate your progress. Are you making the necessary headway toward your goal? Or did you get stuck? If you haven't progressed enough, then you probably need to postpone your goal. Look at this as a learning experience rather than failure. Ask yourself, "I said I would do this, but it hasn't been happening, so what do I need to do differently?"

SHARING YOUR GOALS WITH OTHERS

IN ADDITION TO writing down your goals to make yourself more accountable, tell them to a few people close to you.

Doing so makes it easier to keep making the right choices to meet a particular goal. If you tell your training partner you're going to run your first marathon, it will be easier to keep your running dates together. You don't want your friend to say, "Wait, you're canceling our run? I thought you were training for a marathon."

Telling others your goal will make them want to help you. In the months leading up to the 2014 Boston Marathon, Yordanos would say, "Shouldn't you be sleeping?" when she thought I was staying up too late. Others can remind us to make the choices that will lead to meeting our goals. Even though Yordanos had a tough job taking care of our daughters without my assistance, she understood my goal to win the Boston Marathon. Neither of us questioned my leaving home for 4 weeks of altitude training, because that's what was necessary to achieve the one goal left on my running résumé. Family and friends will also support you when you hit the inevitable rough patches.

I'm not advocating telling the whole world your goal. Stick with a small group of people who you know will care enough to want to help you reach it. With everyone else, underpromise and overdeliver.

Keeping track of your training with a log keeps you focused on your goals. For example, there's no doubt whether your mileage is increasing or decreasing if you write it down every week. That's why I've had a weekly training log since 1993. I gain confidence I'm headed in the right direction every time I write in it. Without a log, you'll have no idea what you've done over the long term.

Committing to Excellence

HAVING A good goal is the first step. Hard work is how you improve yourself to reach that goal; the bulk of this book describes how to add the hard work that has made me a world-class runner to your own training. That hard work doesn't just happen once you set your goal. That comes about only through commitment.

Commitment involves living in a way that makes you better able to work toward meeting your goals. For a professional athlete, that usually means going "all in," completely basing your life on achieving your athletic goals.

That level of commitment isn't necessary (or possible) for most runners. You can, however, be a committed runner in conjunction with the rest of your responsibilities. Doing so means regularly making decisions that contribute to rather than detract from achieving your goal.

For example, say you have a long run scheduled for Saturday morning. Friends ask you to go out Friday night. Commitment is usually going to mean joining them for a short time, maybe having one beer, and

then getting home for a good night's sleep. A lack of commitment would mean frequently staying out late, probably eating and drinking less-than-ideal things, and finding that your long runs are compromised—you cut them short, you're out so late that you don't get started until it's hot, or you skip them altogether.

Situations requiring a decision that will affect your progress come up all the time: when you run, whom you run with, where you run; what you eat, when you eat, how much you eat; how much you sleep; even how you sit at work. Being a committed runner means being aware of these situations and more often than not making a good choice.

One way of knowing that your goal has strong personal meaning is if those types of decisions are easy. Things that might get in the way appear more like obstacles than enticements. If someone else has set your goal for you, you're more likely to take the more immediately appealing route, because deep down you don't really care if you meet that goal. A personally meaningful goal is different from someone giving you an I-bet-you-can't-do-it kind of challenge, such as "I bet you can't run a marathon." Even if you're motivated to prove that person wrong, the ultimate goal is still not coming from within you.

Commitment is a form of risk taking. That's another way of saying there's faith involved in commitment, because you don't know if you're going to reach your goal.

CHOICES, NOT SACRIFICES

MY FORMER MAMMOTH Track Club teammate and fellow Olympic Marathon medalist Deena Kastor likes to say that we make choices, not sacrifices, when we're working toward a goal. I agree with that way of thinking.

The difference might seem like a matter of word choice, but it's an important one. "Sacrifice" has a negative connotation: "Because of my running, I can't do this, I can't do that." Thinking that you're constantly denying yourself in order to meet your goal can make your goal feel like a burden. And who needs more burdens?

"Choice" has a connotation of working toward something that's important to you: "I could do this, but instead I'll choose a different path that will better enable me to meet my goal." Thinking of your decisions as choices, not sacrifices, gives the feeling that you're in control.

For example, when Deena and I were teammates, I lived for most of the year at altitude in Mammoth Lakes, California. My extended family—not to mention great year-round running weather—was several hours away in San Diego. I lived in Mammoth Lakes for 10 years, until I moved to live full-time in San Diego in 2013. I have no regrets about the choice I made to spend a decade in Mammoth Lakes. Being in that setting was what I needed at that time to develop into a world-class athlete. Sure, at times I wondered, "What am I doing here?" But if you don't occasionally question what you're doing, then you're not moving in the right direction. During my time in Mammoth, I won an Olympic silver medal and the New York City Marathon.

Most of the decisions we face when working toward a goal aren't that extreme. They might be as simple as whether to have ice cream or a banana for dessert. (I said simple, not easy!) If part of the way you're working toward your goal is by trying to eat as healthfully as possible, then you can say, "The banana is the best choice for me on this day."

Making the right choices is also made easier by the fact that most goals are finite. You work hard to achieve a goal. After you do, play hard. Take time to recharge physically and mentally. After I won the Boston Marathon, I became extremely busy traveling all around the country. I mostly ate what I wanted when I wanted. My birthday was 2 weeks after Boston, and it seemed like everywhere I went, someone had made me a birthday cake. Especially when I was with my good friend and fellow marathoner Eileen Patrick, who saw what had gone into my Boston win, it was good to just relax and look back on the big accomplishment with a birthday cake. I ran some, but at nowhere near the volume or intensity I did before Boston. After some weeks of this I weighed 132, which is 10 pounds more than I was when I won Boston.

And guess what? I wasn't worried about that. I had wanted to win Boston for years, and I was determined to enjoy having done so. I knew that when it came time to focus on my next goal, the 2014 New York City Marathon, I would return to living like I had before winning Boston. I wound up finishing fourth in New York against a strong field, and I beat the race's course record holder and the Olympic champion. I was very happy with that result, which wouldn't have been possible without again temporarily seeing a banana instead of ice cream as a choice, not a sacrifice.

Improving as a runner doesn't happen overnight. You're going to go through good times and not-so-good times. There will be challenges, obstacles, and setbacks. Aiming for success tests your character. Commitment is the sign that you welcome that test. When you live like that, even if you fall short of your goal, you've passed the test.

When You Don't Meet Your Goals

AS I'LL describe in Chapter 4, Race like Meb, you should have several goals going into a race. Your list should start with your ultimate goal and work downward from there to several potential outcomes that, while not your ultimate aim, are still worthy accomplishments. For example, before the 2014 Boston Marathon, my three top goals were to win, to place in the top three, and to set a personal best. As we'll see in Chapter 4, having a tiered list of goals will motivate you to keep fighting to the finish if it becomes obvious you won't reach your ultimate goal.

In Boston, I was able to reach my ultimate goal for the race: I won. (And I set a personal record, which was a nice bonus.) Meeting your ultimate goal is rare—if you do so all the time, you need to set harder

goals! But not meeting your ultimate goal shouldn't be cause for disappointment. It should give you confidence you're heading in the right direction, and good information about how to proceed. Let me share a few examples to show what I mean.

I was second at the 2004 New York City Marathon and third there in 2005. It was the third-place finish more than the second-place finish that told me I could one day win the race. After all, in 2004, having won the silver medal in the Olympic Marathon 3 months before, I was in fantastic shape. I would have been disappointed if I hadn't made the podium that day.

The 2005 race was a different story. I'd torn my quad muscle during the 10,000-meter race at the world championships that August, 3 months before the marathon. My training for the race was far from ideal. But I was able to stay with the defending champion, Hendrick Ramaala, and the world-record holder, Paul Tergat, until there were just 2 miles to go. That gave me the confidence that if I kept working hard and believing, I could win New York. It took another 4 years, but I became the New York City Marathon champion in 2009—my first marathon victory.

Another example: the 2012 Olympic Marathon, in which I placed fourth. I know some people thought, "Oh, poor guy, one spot out of the medals, the worst place to finish in the Olympics." But with everything that happened to me before and during that race (see Chapter 4 for the details), that was a great result. I was 37 years old at the time, but I'd just placed fourth in the world. That gave me hope that my days as a world-class runner were far from over. I knew that if I could tweak my training to account for being older than most of my competitors, on any given day I could come out on top. Finishing fourth that day in 2012 helped set the stage mentally and physically for winning Boston in 2014.

My previous runs in Boston also helped me win in 2014. In 2006, I ran aggressively from the start, passing halfway in 1:02:44, which was well under course-record pace at the time. I hit the wall hard and finished third in 2:09:56. In 2010, I began to get tightness and irritation in my quad around mile 17 and had to back off. I finished fifth in 2:09:26, with a tear in my left quad. I gave it all I had and felt disappointed I didn't deliver the victory. I felt I let a lot of people down and started to cry as I went past the medical tent. I knew down deep I left nothing on the course.

On the other hand, some people might have said, "He was third, then he was fifth—he doesn't have a chance of winning this race." I had a different takeaway: If I could put it all together and everything clicks for me on race day, then I have a shot at winning.

Some of that thinking stemmed from the fact that in both races the winner broke the course record. In 2010, the winner, Robert K. Cheruiyot, took the course record from 2:07:14 (set in 2006 by a different Robert Cheruiyot) to 2:05:50. I entered the 2010 race with a personal best of 2:09:15.

Afterward, I told myself, "Good for Cheruiyot. That's the fastest anyone has ever run in Boston by almost a minute and a half." I was ready to compete for the win but not to run 2:05, so I couldn't let that affect how I assessed my race. I had made progress on the Boston course—30 seconds faster than in 2006—even though I had quad issues during the last third of the race. And in 2006 I hadn't been patient enough during the first half of the race. I knew there was still a lot of room for improvement in mastering the Boston course and competitors. My faith was rewarded 4 years later when I won Boston in 2:08:37, my fastest marathon ever, and on a tough course when I was almost 39 years old.

Just as the marathon is about patience, life is about overcoming obstacles and having patience. Marathons and other successes teach us delayed gratification. The journey sometimes brings out the best in us. Start with one step at a time, then 1 mile at a time, and you will be surprised by how far you can go.

I believe in what basketball coaching legend John Wooden wrote in *Coach Wooden's Pyramid of Success*. Wooden said success is peace of mind, knowing that you have done the best that you can. If you have given it your best while working toward your goal and been mentally strong in chasing that goal, you have to be satisfied, even if the outcome is short of your ultimate goal. As I like to say, you can reach for the stars, but it's not a bad thing if you land in a cloud.

DOS AND DON'TS OF GOOD THINKING

DO set personally meaningful goals to guide your running.

DO find goals that are challenging but realistic.

DO commit to meeting your goals by regularly making good decisions.

DO share your goals with friends and family who will support you and keep you accountable.

DO view a missed goal as a learning experience.

DON'T set goals that are so vague or easy that they don't motivate you.

DON'T let others set your goals for you.

DON'T set goals that are way beyond your current capabilities.

DON'T think your running goals have to pertain to compotition.

DON'T beat yourself up when you don't meet a goal.

Run like Meb

The importance of good running form and how to get it

RUNNING IS one of the few sports where even serious participants are told not to worry about their technique. You'll hear many people say, "Just run, and your body will find its most efficient form."

I don't agree with that line of thinking. There's room for improvement in everything we do, running mechanics included. A good baseball coach wouldn't tell a hitter, "Just take enough practice swings and you'll be fine." The coach would identify ways in which hitters could get more efficient or slightly reposition themselves to make better use of their ability. The same is true in running.

Why Running Form Is Important

RUNNERS WITH what appears to be bad form have won races and set records. The most famous example in modern times is Paula Radcliffe of Great Britain, who set the still-standing women's world marathon record in 2003. I remember the first time I saw her, at a 10,000-meter track race in Europe. I thought, "There's no way she can win, with her head and neck bobbing around like that." She won. From that I learned that ultimately it's about the engine—your heart and lungs.

My fellow Olympic silver medalist and New York City Marathon champion Priscah Jeptoo of Kenya also has unconventional form for a world-class runner. She appears to run knock-kneed, with her lower legs flicking out to the side with each step. Yet she's been ranked the top marathoner in the world. So it's obvious that the runner with the best form isn't necessarily the best runner.

But that doesn't mean that runners with glitches in their form can't become better than they currently are. Sometimes we inherit bodily quirks that are hardwired into us; it could be disastrous to try to run with a fundamentally different form. But we can always work to improve our weaknesses. My left hand has a tendency to flop out a bit when I run. By being mindful of it and reminding myself to keep it closer to my body, I can run more efficiently.

I'm of the mind-set that if I can run such and such a time with some deficiencies in my form, then I'll run even faster once I figure out how to eliminate them. In the case of someone like Priscah Jeptoo, I think if she raced someone with an equally strong engine but better form, the runner with better form would win.

You can always improve something. How big an improvement you want to make in any area is up to you. But to say, "I'm going to try to be the best runner I can be but ignore my form" is wrong.

THE IMPORTANCE OF CADENCE

ONE ASPECT OF form that's often different between professional runners and those farther back in the pack is cadence, or how many steps are taken per minute. (This is also known as turnover.)

If you watch my competitors and me run by, you'll see we run with good "pop"—we have a quick cadence, with not much ground contact time. Behind us, you'll see more people with a slower cadence; some seem to sink into the ground rather than quickly transitioning to the next step.

Although there's not a set cadence that's good for everyone, I do think that most recreational runners could run more efficiently and be faster if they improved their turnover. You can check your turnover by counting the number of times one foot hits the ground in a minute, then doubling that. Some running watches can also provide that information. If you're regularly below 160 to 165 steps per minute, you would probably benefit from increasing your cadence. (At my solid-but-not-hard pace of about 6 minutes per mile, my cadence is just over 180. When I'm running faster, it can get into the low 200s.)

One of the drills illustrated later in this chapter, Quick Feet, can help increase cadence. It will improve your neuromuscular coordination, which is how well your muscles can execute movements your brain is telling them to do.

When people ask me, "How can I improve my speed?" I tell them to do fartleks. These are short bouts of faster running interspersed with running at your normal pace. For example, over the last couple miles of your normal 7-mile run, alternate 1 minute of faster running with 3 minutes of easier running, or 2 minutes of faster running with 4 minutes of easier running. Or go by landmarks—run fast but controlled to the end of the next block, run easy until you feel recovered, and then pick another landmark to run hard to.

These aren't sprints. Just pick up the pace enough so that your cadence is quicker. You'll get a feel for what it's like to run faster with less ground contact time. That's a better way of working on your cadence than forcing yourself to increase your turnover to hit some desired number of steps per minute. A good time to work on cadence is on a slight downhill, when you can run fast (which we all want to do) and pay attention to your running form.

Nonrunning ways to increase cadence are jumping rope and riding a bicycle or ElliptiGO, which is an elliptical bicycle. They'll get you used to thinking "Quick feet, quick feet, quick feet" and will add pop to your running form.

Simply put, with more efficient form, you'll go farther with each step while using the same amount of energy you'd use running with less efficient form. That will get you to the finish line faster. Also, with your motion better directed toward moving forward, you're less likely to shift some of the

pounding to body parts that aren't designed to absorb it; that should decrease your risk of injury.

It's easy to get thrown off by just one bad element in your running form. For example, if your head is thrust forward of your body rather than being in line with your shoulders and trunk, you might over-stride, lean forward too much, or have longer ground contact time (or all three!). That's going to lead to bringing your hamstring up more behind you than underneath you, which can lead to cramping or injury, as well as being slower.

Any such problems might not be a big deal in a 5-K or a half-marathon (although they probably will make you slower). But over the course of a marathon, you're asking for trouble. Your mechanical weaknesses will be exposed, and they could make you miss your goals.

Also, better running form can simply make running feel easier and more enjoyable. Who wouldn't like to feel better running? The more pleasurable running feels, the more you'll want to do it, and that will lead to improvement.

Finally, I think looking good while you run is important. Most of us draw motivation and satisfaction from positive feedback from others. So just like trying to impress others with your times might help you run faster, trying to impress people with your form can be an incentive to run more efficiently. One of the greatest compliments I've ever received was when Geoffrey Mutai, who holds the Boston and New York City Marathon course records, told me how smooth I look running. It's something that we runners can appreciate about one another, the same way a golfer can appreciate the beauty of a top player's swing.

I've been fortunate to have coaches throughout my career who have emphasized the importance of good form. In high school, we did drills similar to some of the ones described at the end of this chapter, such as A Skip and Quick Feet. In college, at UCLA, we regularly did marching-type drills where we tried to keep accelerating to teach ourselves how to move quickly with good posture. At the beginning of my professional career, I got away from regular form work for a while. But after I recovered from a pelvic stress fracture in 2007 and 2008, I rededicated myself to working on the best possible form. Now I consider it an integral part of my training almost every day.

What Is Good Running Form?

WHILE THERE'S great variation in form among the best distance runners in the world, there are common elements. Here's what some of the key components of good running form look like.

LANDING POSITION. Your feet should land under your center of mass. If you overstride, with your feet landing well in front of you, you'll brake slightly with every step and spend more time on the ground rather than transitioning quickly to the next step.

COMMON PRACTICES THAT CAN THROW OFF YOUR FORM

I SEE A lot of runners who train with their phones strapped on their arms so they can listen to music. This is a bad idea if you care about your running form.

The next time you see someone running like this, take a look. If their phone is on the left arm, above the elbow, you'll see the right hand and arm swinging normally, but the left arm will swing out more because of the extra weight it's carrying.

You might run like this and feel like it doesn't affect you, but you'll have to compensate for that wider arm swing somewhere on your body. Maybe you'll have more side-to-side motion, or your iliotibial band—the ligament running along the outer side of the thigh—will get tight.

I'm not saying it's bad to run with music. But there are ways to do it that won't affect your form, such as clipping a wireless MP3 player to your waistband. And maybe you'll find you enjoy being without your phone during your run, allowing you to disconnect and mentally recharge.

A small fanny pack shouldn't worsen your form too much if you have a few light items in it and keep it right at the center of your back or just above your butt. Be sure it's tightly secured so it doesn't flop and cause you to adjust your stride.

Fuel belts shouldn't affect your form too much, either. As a professional runner, I get to have bottles with my preferred drink waiting for me on the course, usually every 5 kilometers in a marathon. Most runners don't get that perk, and you might want to carry your own if the drink that works for you is different from what is offered on the course.

Now, let's be honest—if you carry a bottle for a 5-K or a 10-K, then we have some problems. But for a marathon or a half-marathon that's going to take more than 2 hours, if carrying your own drink will make you feel comfortable, I'm okay with that.

LEG SWING. Ideally, your leg will drive toward the opposite knee during the swing phase of your stride. Up to the calf is a good goal for people who currently have more of a shuffling stride. Bringing the foot close to the opposite knee means you'll be more upright and covering more ground with each stride, while not overstriding.

STOMACH AND BACK POSITIONS. Keep your midsection engaged, with your stomach tucked in, almost like someone is about to punch you.

ARM CARRIAGE. Swing your arms in the direction you're moving, not back and forth across your body. Imagine that you're going to punch something—you would drive your arm as straight as possible. The insides of your wrists should be near your waist. One way I've been told to visualize this is to think of Old West cowboys reaching for their pistols, with their arms moving quickly past the sides of their waists.

SHOULDER CARRIAGE. Keep your shoulders low and level. Imagine having a long neck

HELPING YOUR FORM THROUGHOUT THE DAY

JUST LIKE SOME of the things we do when we're not running can improve our running form (drills, strengthening, etc.), there are others that can lead to having worse form.

For most runners, that means body positioning during the working hours. Spending many hours a day sitting can lead to worse running form, as your lower back tightens, your shoulders get tense, and your head is thrust forward. Perhaps most harmful, you get what physiotherapist Phil Wharton calls glutes in hibernation, meaning these large muscles that contribute so much to good running form become unused to firing like they should.

One simple way to address this is by getting up from your chair at least twice an hour. Try not to spend more than 1 hour at a time sitting still. Standing or walking around for even a minute can help activate your hibernating muscles.

A standing desk, or a desk with an adjustable height, can help you gradually adjust to spending more time on your feet.

Some runners bring a Swiss ball to work to use as a chair. Sitting on one of these with good posture engages your glutes and core muscles more than using a normal chair does. Whatever you're sitting on, do so with good posture. Try to sit upright with your feet flat on the floor, your legs bent at 90 degrees, and your upper body straight from your waist through your shoulders and head. Your ears should be positioned directly above your shoulders.

One trick I have: If I know I have a meeting where I'm going to have to sit for a long time, I make sure to walk around or at least stand just before it. Plan ahead so that you don't go straight from sitting at your desk to sitting at a conference table. If you're allowed to stand during the meeting, that's great. But you've got to be professional and respect the rules; saying you're standing throughout the meeting because of your running probably won't help your career.

If your job involves a lot of standing with little time to take brief sit-down breaks, try wearing compression socks to help increase blood circulation. If possible, women should avoid high heels, because they can shorten and tighten one's Achilles tendons and calves.

---

with your shoulders down, almost like you're trying to touch the ground rather than the sky.

HEAD CARRIAGE. Imagine that on top of your head there's an egg you don't want to fall off. If you can stay in that posture, with your ears positioned over your shoulders, you're going to have to bring your knee higher to keep your head straight. That will give you a higher cadence and let you cover more ground than you would by overstriding.

With your head held level, look 20 to 30 meters ahead of you, rather than down at your feet or the ground just in front of you. You might look down a little when going uphill or when running on technical trails with frequent obstacles, but otherwise, view things at eye level.

How to Improve Your Running Form

ALTHOUGH I disagree with the idea that your body will find its best form if you run enough, there's no denying that your form will probably improve naturally as you get more experienced. As you get fitter, you're more likely to feel smoother. You'll learn how to better carry yourself so that you get through your increased mileage without cramping or tightness. So if you're relatively new to running or have never run more than a few miles a few times a week, upping your mileage will eventually lead to better form.

Once you have that basic running fitness, form drills can greatly improve how you run. At the end of this chapter you'll see descriptions of the form drills I do regularly. Most of these involve exaggerating one or more elements of good running form. Others help teach you how to improve your stride length or stride rate or both.

I do form drills almost every day. That's how important I think they are. On the day of a race or hard workout, I do them after I've done my warmup jog. On recovery days, I do them after my main run of the day. Usually the only time I don't do drills is the day of a long run.

I realize that most people aren't going to do form drills every day. You might be getting up at 5:00 a.m. to squeeze in your run before reporting to the office by 8:00. Who has time to jump around looking weird? I'll admit to sometimes feeling like that and skipping my drills when I have an early-morning flight.

The best way to make form drills a habit is to plan when you're going to do them and build them into your schedule for those days. As you become familiar with the drills, a session shouldn't take more than 10 minutes. If you feel like you don't have 10 minutes to spare after getting in your run, my advice is to run 1 mile less that day and use the extra time to do drills. (See, I told you I think they're important!) One or two miles less per week for significant improvement in your running form and a lowered injury risk is a great trade-off.

Starting out, shoot to do form drills once a week. As you get more comfortable with them and realize that they don't take much time, add a 2nd day per week. You don't have to do all the drills every time. If you're short on time, commit to doing drills twice a week, including half of the exercises on each of the days. Or concentrate on the ones that most directly address your biggest areas of weakness. If you can sustain that frequency, within a few months you'll notice you're running more efficiently and feeling better while doing so.

You can also do a lot to improve your

FORM CHECKS DURING RACES

PAYING ATTENTION TO your form during a race can help you get to the finish faster.

Starting out, I'm mostly telling myself to relax. Once I'm in a rhythm, I start monitoring: Is my cadence okay? Are my shoulders low? Is my posture good? How am I doing?

I'm always alert for something that feels wrong. Even if I'm feeling great, every 2 or 3 miles I check on my form. I want to make sure I'm running as efficiently as possible. Doing so will help me use less energy, and even just a little extra tension early on can lead to tightness or cramping later.

When I know there's a big hill coming up, I mentally prepare myself to use the proper form for that stretch. That's especially the case when there's a downhill coming up, because I want to make sure I'm ready to switch to a faster turnover.

Late in a race is a great time to focus on your form. Doing so helped me a lot in the last couple miles of the 2014 Boston Marathon. I was extraordinarily tired, the large lead I'd had earlier had been reduced to 6 seconds, and the crowd was going absolutely crazy seeing an American in the lead. I kept telling myself, "Focus, focus, focus. Technique, technique, technique." I concentrated on my form and running as smoothly as possible for little segments, like to the end of the next block or until I caught the next woman (the elite women start before the men). This allowed me to keep pushing on to the finish and the win without tying up or getting distracted.

form during your runs. I monitor and evaluate my form on pretty much every run. I don't mean during the whole run, but every so often I do a body scan to see if I'm running with good form. I also pay attention to whether I feel tightness or discomfort anywhere, because that might indicate there's a flaw somewhere in my form. If something feels off, then I concentrate on that aspect of form for the next little bit of my run.

Don't do this at the beginning of your run. Wait until you're warmed up and in a nice rhythm, then assess how you're carrying yourself and feeling from head to toe. If something seems wrong, for the next 50 or 100 meters, make bettering that your focus. Do you feel bent over at the waist? Practice running more upright, with your stomach tucked and taut. Do your shoulders and neck feel tight? Drop your arms, shake them out, and then concentrate on lowering your shoulders and keeping your head in line with them. Over time, these short-term improvements in form will become more ingrained.

I'm not recommending spending your whole run worrying, "What's wrong with my body?" Instead, look at this feedback as useful information on how you can improve as a runner.

I get extra feedback in two ways when possible. One is when I run past storefront windows. If there are enough windows, I do a full body check: Am I overstriding? Is my chin inching too far forward, or is my head tucked in nicely? Are my arms moving back and forth, with my wrists passing near my waist? If there's just one window and I'm going to get only a short glimpse, I focus on one element of form, such as whether the foot of my trail leg is coming up toward my knee or whether I look aligned versus bent over. When I do these quick window checks, I keep going at the same pace as before the window so I get a read on how I have just been running. The glass enclosures around bus stops are also good places to see your reflection and evaluate your form.

On sunny days, you can also get feedback from your shadow. (I live in San Diego and can do this almost every day; you know what they say about it never raining in Southern California.) The main thing I'm looking for is feedback on my arm swing. I want to see sunlight between my arms and my back; that tells me I'm swinging my arms enough and that they're working in sync with a long, fluid stride. But if I don't see that triangle formed by the shadows of my upper arm, lower arm, and torso, then I know I need to open my arm swing a little more.

Again, you don't want to be doing all this form checking all the time and winding up with a stiff neck. Have fun on your runs! But you need just a few seconds to evaluate how you're doing and what you might be able to do better. After a while, these quick scans become a habit and an integral part of becoming a better runner.

The Role of Shoes in Running Form

SHOES ARE important in regard to form in two main ways.

First and most basic, if your shoes don't fit properly, your form is going to be thrown off.

You don't want your feet to be irritated or constricted in any way that will alter your mechanics. That's true not just as you start your run but also in the later miles. That's when blisters can form from a bad fit, and you'll be forced to land differently than your body naturally wants to.

Good fit without constriction is especially important for marathoners. Our feet tend to swell over the many miles of a marathon. That could lead to hot spots and blisters just when it's getting much more difficult to run with good form, even without shoe issues.

Second, you want the features of a shoe to encourage rather than fight against your natural form. Your shoes should feel like extensions of your feet when you run. Another way of saying that is that the shoes should more or less get out of the way and let you run; you shouldn't be thinking about them constantly, like "These feel rigid" or "These make me feel like I'm on a pogo stick." Different runners have different

THE BEST USES OF BEING BAREFOOT

BEING BAREFOOT CAN be a beautiful thing. Who doesn't like to run into the water at the beach or feel the grass beneath you in a nice park? Especially now that I live in San Diego, I love chasing my daughters at the beach or park barefoot.

But I don't agree with running barefoot on pavement. Of course, people can do what they want. But are you really going to feel comfortable running barefoot on the road? Are you really going to be able to run your best when you're worrying about every step you're taking? I don't know of any elite runners who currently run barefoot on hard surfaces. That's not because we have shoe contracts—if regular barefoot running on the roads helped performance, we would do it.

I think it's good to go barefoot occasionally on the right surfaces. I sometimes do post-run striders on grass to see how my foot is landing. You can do this to see what your natural foot strike is; when running barefoot, are you a heel striker, midfoot striker, forefoot striker? Once you know that, you can use this information to guide your shoe choices, selecting running shoes that encourage you to run with that type of foot strike.

Little bits of barefoot running on grass can also strengthen the small muscles in your feet. I and other elite runners do short cooldown jogs on the inside, soft perimeter of a track after a hard workout. I also like to walk around the house barefoot as a way to strengthen my foot muscles.

needs along the spectrums of stability and cushioning; work with knowledgeable staff at a running store to find models that best match your form and body.

That said, I think most runners are best served by a neutral (not too rigid, not too flexible), lightweight shoe with good but not excessive cushioning. The shoe made by my shoe sponsor, Skechers, that fits that bill is the Meb Strada. It's an example of the modern neutral cushioned shoe—it has enough cushioning and comfort to see you through lots of miles but, at about 10 ounces, it's considerably lighter than similar shoes of 5 years ago, thanks to advances in materials and manufacturing processes. All running shoe brands have at least one model of this type.

The Meb Strada is also a good example of how, over the last 5 years, the heel-to-toe drop, the difference in height between the highest part of the back of the shoe and the highest part of the front of the shoe, has decreased in most shoes. I think this is a good development. Too much heel-to-toe drop can tip you forward, encourage a more severe heel strike, and interfere with running form in other ways.

Minimalist shoes have gotten a lot of attention in recent years. Heel-to-toe drop has been one part of shoe design that people interested in minimalist running have focused on. Like I said, I think it's good that the standard shoe has a smaller heel-to-toe drop than was the case 10 years ago. But I don't agree that a few millimeters of heel-to-toe drop, or a little difference in a shoe's stack height (how high off the ground it puts your feet), is going to affect your running form so much that you're suddenly going to be a lot faster. Ultimately, commitment and training are what get you to the finish line.

I think the best use of minimalist shoes is to wear them for short runs or when doing striders to get feedback on your form and some of the benefits of barefoot running without having to worry about cutting your feet. But I recommend against wearing the barely-there shoes for all your running, especially once you get past 35 or 40 miles a week. You might be able to get away with doing 10- or 15-mile runs in them for a year or two, but eventually the pounding and lack of cushioning can aggravate your plantar fascia (the ligament running along the bottom of your foot, connecting your heel and toes), Achilles tendon, and foot bones.

I'd rather runners get the fundamentals of good form down by having good running-specific strength and flexibility and by regularly doing the form drills described on the next page.

RUNNING FORM DOS AND DON'TS

DO regularly work to improve your running form.

DO consider form drills an integral part of training.

DO practice elements of good form for short periods during some runs.

DO monitor your form during races to stay efficient.

DO consider how your posture when you're not running affects your form.

DON'T overstride!

DON'T force changes in your running form.

DON'T work on your form so much that you don't enjoy your running.

DON'T think that shoes are a magic bullet for improving form.

DON'T forget that training and desire are what ultimately get you to the finish line.

Running Form Drills

The following drills will improve your running form in many ways—by strengthening key running muscles, by improving your range of motion via exaggerating some aspects of the running gait, by improving the communication between your nervous system and muscles, and simply by making you more mindful of good running form.

I do running form drills almost every day. As I said earlier in this chapter, I understand that you might not have the time to match my frequency. But aim to do drills at least twice a week, even if doing so means cutting your run a mile short on those days. The payoff with the time invested—greater speed and less injury risk—outweighs what you'll get from another couple of miles for the week.

You don't have to do all these drills every time. Rotate among the exercises, emphasizing those that best address the aspects of your running form that you need the most help with.

These three skipping exercises increase stride length and knee lift and improve single-leg balance.

A Skip, Forward and Backward

Move forward in a skipping motion by raising your knees to a 90-degree angle, or as high as possible, while the bottom of your raised leg's foot stays parallel with the ground. Pump your arms in sync with your legs while staying tall and relaxed in your upper body. The key is to drive the raised leg down into the ground to initiate the knee lift of the opposite leg.

Go 20 yards, rest briefly, then go another 20 yards. Once you're familiar with the drill, do 20 yards forward, then 20 yards backward.

B Skip, Forward and Backward

In contrast to A Skip, in which your feet are parallel to the ground, in B Skip you partly tuck the foot of your raised leg under your butt, then swing it out to extend your hamstring before the foot contacts the ground at midfoot. As in A Skip, use the landing of the raised leg to propel the other leg.

Go 20 yards, rest briefly, then go another 20 yards. Once you're familiar with the drill, do 20 yards forward, then 20 yards backward.

C Skip, Forward and Backward

From the same starting position, quickly snap your raised foot back as if you're trying to kick your butt, while keeping your supporting leg straight. Use the landing of one leg to power the start of the movement on the other leg. Concentrate on how quickly you bring your feet up and back.

Go 20 yards, rest briefly, then go another 20 yards. Once you're familiar with the drill, do 20 yards forward, then 20 yards backward.

These next three drills will lessen your ground contact time and give you a quicker, more efficient turnover. Carioca drills also improve your knee lift and hips' range of motion.

Carioca

Move laterally at a skipping pace. Move to the left with your left leg straight, while your right leg alternates crossing your left leg from behind and in front. Throughout the motion, swivel your hips and swing your arms across your body. Go 20 yards in one direction. Turn 180 degrees and go 20 yards in the other direction, keeping your right leg straight and your left leg moving behind and across your right leg.

Carioca with High Knees

Do the basic Carioca drill, but now try to cross your right leg over your left knee as you're moving to the left. Swing your right leg behind you and repeat. Go 20 yards in one direction. Turn 180 degrees and go 20 yards in the other direction, crossing your left leg over your right knee.

Quick Feet

Staying on the balls on your feet, shuttle forward as quickly as possible while skimming over the ground inches at a time. Keep your knee lift to a minimum. Do twice for 10 yards each time.

The next few drills teach your running muscles to work in sync with each other, increase your power when pushing off, improve your ability to move in all three planes of motion, and strengthen several often-neglected muscles.

Double-Leg Bounce, Forward and Backward

Stand tall. Lifting simultaneously from your ankles, knees, and core, reach for the sky while bouncing forward on both legs. Move forward just a few inches at a time. Go 10 feet forward, then 10 feet backward.

Single-Leg Lateral Bounce, to Both Sides

Stand with your right leg straight and your left leg bent, with your left foot by your right calf. Hop to the side on your right leg, going a few inches at a time. Go 10 feet in one direction, then 10 feet in the other direction. Repeat in both directions using your left leg.

Single-Leg Bounce, Forward and Backward

Bounce forward in the same way as in the Double-Leg Bounce, but use only one leg at a time. Hop with your hopping leg slightly bent, the raised leg bent at a 90-degree angle, and the foot of the raised leg near the knee of the hopping leg. If keeping your foot there is too challenging, keep it near the ankle of the hopping leg. Go 10 feet forward, then 10 feet backward, on each leg.

Soccer Ball Kick (With Imaginary Soccer Ball)

Stand with both legs straight. Keeping your left foot on the ground, raise your right leg slightly and hold it a few inches forward of your body. Now imagine kicking or dribbling a soccer ball with your right foot for a few seconds. Switch legs and do the Imaginary dribble with your left foot. Do 5 times with each foot.

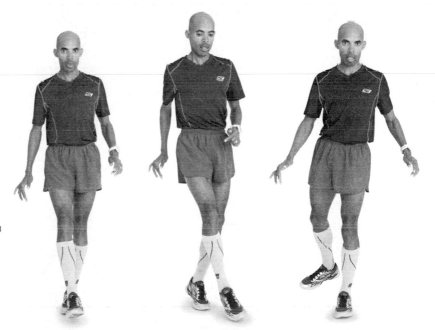

*Lunges build strength throughout
your core and improve your balance.*

Forward Walking Lunge

At a slow walking pace, lift one knee to 90 degrees before taking a step forward with it and landing with your knee remaining at a 90-degree angle. Leave the other foot rooted in its original spot. Push from the glutes of your forward, bent leg to initiate the forward lunge of the other leg. Do for 20 yards.

Backward Walking Lunge

Use the same sequence of motions as the forward lunge but while walking backward. Don't get frustrated if you initially find this difficult. Do for 20 yards.

Lateral Crossover Lunge

Stand on your left leg. Bring your right foot by your left knee, and then cross your right foot behind your left leg while squatting as low as you can to the left. Bring your right leg back over, and stand on it to repeat the exercise in the other direction. Do 10 times in each direction.

Doing the following drills on a slight grade of 1 or 2 percent increases your power gains (uphill drills) and turnover and agility gains (downhill ones). If you can't find a suitable hill that's convenient, do them on level ground—better to do them there than to not do them!

Ankle Dribble on Slight Downhill

Run down the hill, but cover only inches with each step. Don't worry about your speed. Focus on staying tall while bringing your feet only as high as the ankle of the opposing leg. Do for 10 yards.

Bound for Distance on Slight Uphill

Use the basic lunge motion described in Forward Walking Lunge but at more of a running pace. Lean forward a little bit and push off with the grounded leg as forcefully as possible for maximum forward distance. Go 10 yards.

Hopscotch on Slight Uphill

Stand with your knees slightly bent, as if you're cross-country skiing. While keeping your legs bent, jump from one side to the other, moving about 1 foot forward at a time. Do for 10 yards.

Bent-Knee Skip on Slight Uphill

Skip up the hill with your upper body as straight and erect as possible. Imagine your glutes and knees working together to propel the motion. Land on your midfoot. Skip uphill for 10 yards.

Toe Lunge on Slight Downhill

Imagine looking at a pair of scissors spread out. Try to make that shape with your body by moving down the hill with a full stride, with your legs spread out and your arms swinging back and forth. Land on your forefoot and push off quickly. Lunge downhill for 10 yards.

Bound for Height on Slight Uphill

Use the basic lunge motion as in Bound for Distance, but stay as tall and upright as possible. Push off with the grounded leg as forcefully as possible for maximum height on each step. Do for 10 yards.

Lateral drills engage important gluteal muscles and improve your sideways balance, which is especially important when you're running on uneven footing, such as trails and banged-up roads.

Lateral Bent-Knee Walk

Position yourself as if you're sitting on a chair, with your feet and knees pressed together. Maintain the imaginary sitting position while walking sideways for 20 yards in one direction, then 20 yards in the other direction.

Lateral Bent-Knee Crossover

Start in the imaginary sitting position, but with your legs shoulder-width apart. Cross your left foot over your right foot, then move your right leg to the right by about a foot. Walk 20 yards to the right this way, then walk 20 yards in the other direction, leading with your left leg while crossing your right foot over your left foot.

Lateral Bent-Knee Double Crossover

Start in the same position as for the Lateral Bent-Knee Crossover. But when crossing your left foot over your right foot, alternate moving it in front of and behind your right foot. Walk 20 yards to the right this way, then walk 20 yards in the other direction, leading with your left leg while crossing your right foot over your left foot.

These final two drills illustrate the importance of good arm movement when you're running. They're especially useful if your arms tend to go sideways across your body rather than straight back and forth when you run.

Standing Quick Arms

Stand tall with your legs straight, looking straight ahead. Swing your arms rapidly as if you're running, with your wrists passing near your waist and your shoulders relaxed. Notice how your legs want to start moving once your arms are moving well. Do for 30 seconds.

Sitting Quick Arms

Sit on the ground with your legs straight out in front of you and your back straight. Swing your arms as if you're running; concentrate on not letting your arms go across your upper body. Do for 30 seconds.

Train like Meb

The principles
and types
of runs that
lead to success

RUNNERS LOVE to talk about training, so let's get right into it. This chapter describes my overall training principles and the basic types of runs I do and shows how to put them together in a good training plan. By the end of this chapter, you'll have a solid understanding of how to implement the basic elements of my running program.

Training Principles

REGARDLESS OF things like how much you run and whether you have a favorite race distance, good training programs have several things in common. Below are key principles that I've had success with throughout my career.

IT'S BETTER TO BE UNDERTRAINED THAN OVERTRAINED. As runners, we tend to think more is always better. We all want to be known for going the extra mile.

At times, that used to be me, but not these days. In my own running and that of many elite and recreational runners, I've seen more problems arise from going 1 mile too many than 1 too few. Of course, when you're striving for personal excellence, you have to take risks and push your boundaries. But you don't want to push those boundaries past their breaking point. A few weeks of great training isn't going to help you on race day if you get hurt and never make it to the start line.

Learn to tell the difference between acceptable short-term fatigue and the lingering fatigue that can lead to performance decreases and injury. The normal fatigue from working hard shouldn't interfere with progressing in your training. Sure, you're going to have days when you're dragging, but you'll usually find you can run the distance and/or pace you want once you get going. The kind of fatigue that has you sore all the time and running slower even though you're working harder is what you want to avoid.

Not overreaching is also a good principle for individual workouts. I've never been a hands-on-my-knees or pass-me-the-vomit-bucket guy. Back when we worked together at UCLA, Bob Larsen, my longtime coach, instilled in me that you should leave a workout being able to do more. Sometimes during a track session, I'd want to do another mile repeat, and Coach Larsen would say, "No, we've done enough for today. Go do your cooldown." You should always feel you could have done another interval or a longer tempo run or another mile or two on your long run. You should never feel like you're so tired you can't even walk straight. This is especially the case when your goal race is soon. Making it to the start line healthy and strong is your top priority then.

In some ways, the fitter you get, the harder it can be to restrain yourself. You get more efficient and have greater work capacity, so any one run doesn't take that much out of you. As I'm getting near racing shape, I often have to remind myself, "Hold back, hold back." I don't want to look back 2 weeks later and realize that the day when I went the extra mile or unnecessarily pushed the pace was when my hamstring started bothering me.

An idea I described in Chapter 1—under-promise and overdeliver—applies to workouts. I've trained with some people who have left their best races in workouts. Based on the training I saw them do, they should have run up to a minute faster in short races and 4 to 5 minutes faster in marathons than they did. If you regularly do workouts that point to your having the ability to run certain times in races but you don't achieve those times, back off a bit on the intensity and/or volume of your hard sessions. You should be pleasantly tired and eager for a recovery day after hard workouts, but you shouldn't be exhausted. Save the racing for race day.

I've also known runners whose training logs for any 1- or 2-week span have looked more impressive than mine. They could almost never sustain that level of training but, understandably, thought they could really break through only if they worked as hard as possible. Usually, they got hurt. If they didn't get injured, they didn't race up to their expectations, which made them resolve to work that much harder. Recovery is an integral part of training, which is why I've devoted an entire chapter of this book to the subject.

WHEN WORKOUTS ARE GOING GREAT

SOMETIMES IN HARD workouts you find you're running even faster than planned. What to do in those rare but wonderful instances depends on when the race is.

If it happens when I have an important race within the next week, such as a Tuesday workout before a Sunday race, I hold back. Even if you feel great, a faster-than-usual workout can increase your injury risk, and you might not be fully recovered by race day. Why chance it? Stay focused on the real goal, which is that upcoming race.

If I don't have a race coming up soon, I let it rip. That's my body telling me it feels great that day. If you feel amazing and really want to push, you might as well, because that's what (you hope) it will be like on race day. To me, this is the same as backing off the pace when you don't feel great, in that in both instances you're listening to your body. Just be sure to take a good recovery day after one of these feel-great days. As basketball coaching legend John Wooden said, it's not what you do in the 2 hours of practice but how you take care of yourself the next 22 hours.

PROGRESS PATIENTLY, WITH SMALL STEPS. At the beginning of my professional career, I was fortunate to meet the great Kenyan runner Paul Tergat, who won two Olympic silver medals and five world cross-country titles and is a former world-record holder at 10,000 meters and the marathon.

I asked Paul how he trained. What were his workouts like? His long runs? His weekly mileage? What did I need to do to be as good as him?

WHO SHOULD RUN MARATHONS?

I WOULD NEVER tell anyone they should run a marathon. (But if someone asks, I'll recommend they do one at some point in their life.) I know lots of daily runners who do more mileage than a lot of marathoners, but they're just not interested in a 26.2-mile race. They don't have to prove anything to anyone.

I would also not tell people not to run a marathon, even if they've really never run before. If someone has that commitment, what that person needs is guidance on how to prepare. Ideally, they'll commit to a marathon that's several months away and slowly build their endurance through a combination of walking and running. If they have a positive experience, maybe they'll want to try another marathon and will be able to train a little harder. Or maybe they'll say, "Once is enough, but I discovered I like running, and I am going to keep doing it a few days a week." Either way is fine with me. The important thing is that the person remains a runner.

He put his arm around me and said, "Meb, I could give you my workouts, what to do or what not to do. You might survive for 2 weeks, and then you're going to crash, because we're on different levels right now. Just keep working hard and be patient, and you're going to be a good runner."

I learned from that to make progress in small amounts. I kept working hard, but not so hard that I got hurt or burned out and couldn't build on previous accomplishments. Two years after Paul and I met, I was able to make the same Olympic 10,000-meter final as him. I finished far behind him in that

race, but set a personal best. By the 2004 Olympic Marathon, I felt ready to race him, even though his best was more than 5 minutes faster than mine. I won the silver medal while Paul finished 10th. That was possible only because I'd taken his advice—I gradually worked my way up to being one of the best marathoners in the world. If I had tried to copy Paul's training in 1998, I wouldn't have won an Olympic medal 6 years later.

Always base your training goals on where you are now. Don't try to mimic what you read or hear others are doing—you don't know how long it took them to get to that level. By regularly aiming a little higher, you can keep progressing. Over the course of just a few training cycles, you'll significantly advance what you're capable of.

CONSISTENCY IS KING. When I tell people you don't lose much aerobic fitness in 3 weeks off from running, I don't mean that's how you improve. Perhaps more than any other sport, running rewards regularity. Implicit in patiently making small amounts of progress is training consistently.

There are physical and psychological obstacles to consistency. If you're unable to maintain the running schedule you want to because of constant soreness or strains, that's a sign you're trying to do too much for your current capability. You need to run fewer times per week or do some of your runs slower or reduce the distance of your runs. Simultaneously, you should be working on improving your strength and

RUNNING TWICE A DAY

MOST ELITE RUNNERS run twice a day most days of the week. Doing so is a better way to run high mileage than aiming for the same volume on one run a week, because you space out the pounding and can get more of a training effect. On a typical "double" day, I do my main run of the day, such as a hard workout or a 10-mile recovery run, in the morning, and then a shorter, easier run, such as 4 miles, in the afternoon. Ten years ago, I doubled 6 days a week. These days, it's more like 3. As I describe in Chapter 8, I've replaced some of my second, shorter runs with an ElliptiGO ride or complete rest.

I think there's a role for running twice a day for some runners doing much lower mileage than elites. For example, take someone who runs 50 miles a week by running 10 miles 5 days a week. If that person has the time, I would advise splitting those runs two or three times a week, so that some days are 5 miles in the morning and 5 miles in the evening. It might seem counterintuitive, but doing so should lower injury risk because you're spreading out the pounding over the course of the day.

Also, it's when we get tired that our running mechanics can deteriorate enough to make us more susceptible to injury. If a typical 10-miler takes you 85 minutes, that's a long time to be out there every time you run. You might be able to maintain better form on two runs of 40 and 45 minutes.

Another good day for doubling is a recovery day. This, too, might seem counter to common sense. But think about a situation such as doing a track workout on a Tuesday night after work, and then getting up early the next morning to run 10 miles before work. That's cramming a lot of work into a short time. The day after your track workout, the goal is to get in some easy miles that will set you up for your next hard or long run. You might better achieve that goal by splitting that day's mileage into something like 4 miles in the morning and 6 miles in the evening.

If you're getting ready for a longer race, like a 10-miler, half-marathon, or marathon, then I don't think you should be doing a lot of doubles until you're running at least 55 miles a week. For those races, you want the strength that comes from longer once-a-day runs. But you could still benefit from occasionally running twice a day, such as in the recovery-day scenario described above.

flexibility (see Chapters 6 and 7) so your body can better hold up to the amount of running you're trying to do.

I more often hear from runners who lack consistency because they have a hard time remaining motivated. They might get fired up about running for 2 weeks, then lose interest and barely run for 2 weeks, and repeat this cycle several times a year. In this case, the solution usually is: Put your running shoes on and get out the door. It really is that simple most of the time. Once you warm up and start sweating, you'll be glad you made the effort to run. Remember that feeling the next time you feel like running just doesn't appeal to you that day. You're almost always going to be happy you ran, and you're almost never going to be happy you missed a day when you had planned to run.

If you struggle with consistency, get some training partners. Even if you don't feel

RUNNING STREAKS AND DAYS OFF

ALTHOUGH I HAVE running logs dating back to high school, I don't know what my longest streak of consecutive days running is. I've definitely never run every day for a year.

I don't know what my longest streak is because that's not something that's important to me. I have some friends who have streaks measured in years, and I admire their commitment. Most runners channel their type A behavior toward other goals. For me, that's competition. And to do your absolute best in competition, I think you need days off from running when they're merited.

I always take a break after a marathon. In the first few days after, I don't have a choice—I can barely walk. Depending on how beat up I am and when my next important race is, I might do almost no running for as long as 3 weeks. I believe you can miss 3 weeks of running and lose almost no aerobic fitness. You'll feel creaky, less efficient, and probably heavier when you get going again, but those feelings go away quickly. So if I race two marathons a year, right there that's a large number of days off from running.

I've known elite marathoners who have tried to return to normal training soon after a great race. They're fired up and want to keep building on their fitness. They've almost always run into problems when they've done that instead of taking a short break to really recover and then building back into their training.

Over the years, I have, unfortunately, missed many days of running because of injury. While I wish I hadn't missed those days, I know that not running was the correct decision. Taking time off to let the injury heal meant that I was back to normal training sooner than if I'd kept running.

I also take days off not because of injury but just because of a muscular strain or something else feeling "off" more than it should. I'll think back to how more serious injuries might have felt like this when they

started and decide 1 day off now is better than 10 later. Definitely don't run on days when one of these little flare-ups will change your running form. I'm usually fine after taking one of these nip-it-in-the-bud rest days.

I don't run when I'm sick. I've always had a very low count of white blood cells, which is what your body uses to fight viruses, infections, etc. So when I get sick, I get really sick. I get a high fever and am crashed on the couch. I'm always amazed that 3 days earlier I was doing a tempo run at 5 minutes per mile, and now I can barely move around the house. Deciding not to run on those days is a no-brainer. In cases of less severe illness, use your judgment. If you have an important race coming up, don't run. Focus on getting better so you can resume training as soon as possible. If you're a long way away from an important race and aren't terribly sick, a short, slow run probably won't make things worse. But it's also probably not going to help you get better sooner.

I almost never take days off because I feel rundown (as opposed to when I'm sick). Because I'm so dedicated to recovery, it's rare that I feel like I have no energy. There are certainly times I feel sluggish, but once I get going on my run, I'm fine.

I now occasionally take days off that 10 years ago I would have run on in a similar situation. For example, if I have a travel day that starts early, and I'm unfamiliar with my destination and it's already been a 12-hour day by the time I can run, I'm okay with missing that day. I might take a nap instead. Sure, I could get out for a short run, but if I feel I'll be better off later in the week for having rested, I'll do so and not feel guilty about it.

When I'm home and decide to take a day off because of a little ache or pain, I try to do things that I usually don't do when I'm training. I might go have a coffee or go to the library, and I get to spend more time with my family. Enjoy those days instead of sitting around feeling guilty about not running.

WHEN WORKOUTS ARE GOING BADLY

SOME HARD WORKOUTS are a struggle from the start. You feel bad warming up, and your times are slower than you want them to be. Should you cut the workout short because your body is telling you today isn't the day to run hard, or should you stick it out?

I almost always finish the workout in those situations. My times aren't what I'd hoped for, but I'm getting the effort in. If later that day I feel even worse, I might not run the next day and hope to rebound quickly. (This is different from cutting a workout short because you feel an injury coming on. In that case, you should stop the workout; your long-term health is more important than a few more intervals.) I play whatever mind games I need to play to get through the workout. For example, if I'm doing mile repeats and I'm getting a little slower on each one, I'll focus on my average for the session. So instead of thinking, "I started at 4:35, then ran 4:38, then 4:41; this is just getting worse and worse," I'll tell myself, "You're averaging 4:38. Now how close to that can you get on this next one?"

Always consider why your times are slower. It might be hot or windy, or you haven't slept well the last couple of nights, or you've been really busy at work. Take it one interval at a time, or 1 mile at a time on a tempo run, and get through the workout as best you can.

What I've done more often than cutting a workout short is not starting it in the first place. Say it's the day before I've planned a tempo run, and I still don't feel recovered from my last hard or long run. If I feel I'm more tired than I should be, I'll postpone the tempo run.

I've even made that decision while warming up before a hard workout. It's a matter of knowing your body and being honest with yourself: "If I go hard today, will I dig myself into a hole? Or am I just a little off, in which case it probably won't be one of my best workouts, but gutting it out isn't going to set me back?" I usually go ahead with the workout. In fact, I've had some of my best hard sessions when I felt horrible warming up and thought, "It's going to be a long day at the office." That's the beauty of doing a thorough warmup.

like running that day, once you get there, the energy's positive and you'll get the run done. Making yourself accountable to others is a sign of commitment, not weakness. Nearly all elite runners train with others. Even though I do most of my running by myself these days, I have friends who pace me on a bike on my long and hard runs.

Consistency doesn't mean you run every day no matter what. (See "Running Streaks and Days Off" for examples of when I don't run.) Instead, consistency is about running frequently enough that it's a regular part of your life. For some people, that's every day, while for others it's three times a week.

VARIETY IS THE SPICE OF RUNNING. If you want to run the same distance at the same pace over the same course on every run, I'm fine with that. But you'll make greater gains in fitness by mixing things up, with different days having different emphases. More well-rounded training is essential if you want to race anywhere near your best. And if you're like most runners, you'll find that variety in how far and hard you run keeps things more interesting, meaning that you'll be more motivated to be consistent.

A lot of running injuries are repetitive stress injuries—a weak point in your body can no longer hold up to the pounding.

One way to reduce injury risk is by varying the stress. Running faster some days and slower others will mean running with slightly different form, depending on how fast you're going. Running longer some days and shorter others will mean that on some days you'll have much less pounding than if you run the same distance every day. Running hilly courses some days and flatter courses others, or on hard surfaces some days and soft surfaces others, will mean varying the muscular requirements compared to running the same course every day.

Like I said, great variety within a typical training week is crucial to racing your best. Unlike a lot of recreational runners, I rarely have weeks where I do medium-intensity, medium-length runs several days in a row. My hard days are hard, and my easy days are easy. Long runs extend my endurance, and short, slow runs help me recover for the next long or hard run. Different types of workouts work different energy systems so that I'm not lacking in any area.

Variety will improve your running even if you have no racing plans. Small bits of faster running once a week, or once every 2 weeks, will add a fun challenge and improve your running form. I don't mean going to the track for grueling intervals or doing long tempo runs on a measured course. On days when you feel good after a mile or 2, throw in some surges, like 1 minute of hard running followed by 2 minutes of easy running, repeated four, six, or eight times, whatever feels good. I don't mean you should sprint; just pick up the pace by maybe a minute per mile. Maybe a week later when you feel like running hard again, do the first mile or 2 slow, then gradually pick up the pace so that you run the middle 2 or 3 miles at a strong pace, but one at which you can still talk. Then use the last part of your run as a nice, easy cooldown. I think you'll find you finish these runs with a great sense of satisfaction. They might pique your interest enough that you'll want to add more variety and maybe even consider racing.

Another important form of variety is within individual runs. One big difference between the training of elite and recreational runners is the range of paces on a standard run. When I tell people I start my runs at 6:45 to 7:00 per mile, they think, "What? No way—I could keep up with you for a mile or 2."

But it's true. Ever since high school, I've started slowly and picked up the pace over the course of the run. ("Slow" is a relative term, but 7 minutes per mile is more than 2 minutes per mile slower than my marathon pace.) I let my body tell me what pace it's comfortable at on nonworkout runs. Starting out, that's slower than 20 minutes later, when my muscles are warm and I've loosened up.

That's different from how a lot of recreational runners do their regular runs. Within a few minutes they're at the pace they'll more or less hold for the rest of the run. Or they might do the opposite of my start-slow–finish-faster method and finish a

GPS UNITS AND OTHER GADGETS

I RUN WITH a smartwatch every day, including during road races. I like looking at all the data—distance, average pace, mile splits, heart rate, stride length, ground contact time, calories burned, and more.

At the same time, however, I listen to my body first. What I see on the watch is more confirmation of what I am feeling than something that dictates what I do. For example, at the beginning of a training cycle, I might do a 10-mile run at an average heart rate of 135 to 140. Two months later, when I'm nearing racing shape, I might have an average heart rate closer to 120 for the same run at the same pace. Of course, I would have been able to tell you even without the heart rate data that I was fitter. But it's nice to get that reassurance.

I download the data and sometimes look back at them in the same way that I look at old handwritten training logs. It can be good to see things like what the data looked like 2 months before I won Boston and whether they are similar to my current data, so I can tell whether my training is moving in the right direction.

At home I usually run the same few courses, which I mapped out long ago. When traveling I find the GPS function really valuable. I'm one of those runners who like to see nice round numbers, like 10.0 miles instead of 9.8 or 10.2 miles. Deep down, I know it all evens out over time. That's just how I'm wired. Along those lines, I'm a numbers guy and like being able to look at my mile splits for runs and compare them to how I felt during the run.

To repeat what I said above about starting slow and finishing faster, it's not a good idea to have set paces you tell yourself you "should" be running in training. Don't constantly look at your watch and pick up the pace just because you see a time you think is too slow. Let your body dictate the right pace for whatever effort you want to run that day. Let the data be an objective record of your subjective running experience. Over time, you'll find they get closer and closer.

lot slower than they started. That means you've been fighting your body the whole way. Gradually letting the pace come to you will result in the same or a faster overall time for your run than being at the same pace from the start, and it's a more natural way to run. I'll say a lot more about this in Chapter 9, when I detail recovery runs.

BE A STUDENT OF THE SPORT. The fact that you're reading this book shows that you're interested in learning more about running. There's great value in seeing what accomplished runners have done, looking for common threads and figuring out how to apply their methods to your running.

I started being curious about how others train when I was in high school, and that continued through my meeting Paul Tergat in 1998 and up to today. There are always new things to learn in any field. I try not only to observe what others have done to succeed but also to learn from others' mistakes. For example, being a student of the sport led me to the 9-day training cycle I used before winning the Boston Marathon.

There's always a balance between taking others' advice and doing what's best for you. Just like we all have different fingerprints, we all come to running as unique athletes. The basic principles of training apply to almost all runners, but the best way to implement them can vary widely. For example, some runners thrive on a lot of endurance work, while others respond best to shorter, faster workouts. I always weigh my observations against what I know has and hasn't worked for me and what my fitness level currently is. I keep an open mind while remaining skeptical of claims that one person's approach is exactly what all runners should do.

Part of being a student of the sport is being a student of your own running. I've kept a running log since high school. It's been a great help in finding patterns that have led to my best races or worst injuries. These days, my older logs can also be a source of motivation. I might do a tempo run on a course I know I ran on 8 years ago, and then see how I compare now to then. I've seen differences as small as a few seconds. I get a huge confidence boost from seeing that I'm running as fast now in workouts as I was in my early 30s.

My logs are very detailed, especially now that I download data from my smartwatch. I include distance, pace, course, and notes about anything that might have affected the workout, such as weather or a poor night's sleep. I also note how I felt, both in terms of energy level and whether any body part was bothering me. A good log has enough information in it so that you can notice patterns, such as at what level of mileage you start to get too tired or sore or what sequence of long runs and workouts leads to your best races.

WHERE TO DO LONG RUNS

MY TYPICAL LONG run is on a mix of hard and soft surfaces. For example, at home I have a 7.5-mile loop that's mostly on grass but includes 1.5 to 2 miles of asphalt. For a really long run, I'll do that loop three times, then finish with a few more miles on pavement. So in a marathon-length long run, about 9 miles are on a hard surface.

This approach makes more sense to me than doing the whole run on pavement, which would make me sorer. I do my tempo runs and intervals on hard surfaces. Between that and the portion of my long run on pavement, especially at the end, I'm adequately prepared to handle the pounding of a marathon. I'm always balancing the specific needs of an upcoming race with the overall goal of staying healthy.

If you're not training for a marathon, do your long run on whatever surface you like.

The Building Blocks of a Good Training Program

LIKE I said, I have a lot of variety in the types of runs I do in a typical training week (or, these days, 9-day training cycle). Even if you don't plan to race soon, regularly doing different types of runs will get you fitter and keep running more interesting. At the start

A TEMPO RUN AT ALTITUDE BEFORE THE 2014 NEW YORK CITY MARATHON.

of a training cycle, or if you've never done several types of workouts, build a good foundation with 4 to 5 weeks of steady running. Then begin to add variety with one high intensity workout per week.

Here's a brief description of the main types I've done during my career, with an emphasis on the ones I currently do the most. I have a lot to say about long runs, because that's what other runners most often ask me about.

LONG RUNS. Long runs are primarily about covering the distance. I'm not saying to jog them, but they shouldn't be so hard that you're trashed afterward and spend the rest of the week recovering. I start mine at an easy pace and gradually get faster as I warm up. By the end I'm usually running close to a minute per mile faster than I was at the beginning.

My exact pace varies, depending on how hilly the course is and whether I'm running at altitude. But generally speaking, for the bulk of my long runs I'm going a little over 1 minute per mile slower than my marathon race pace. For example, one of my long runs before the 2014 Boston Marathon was 26.2 miles in 2:36; that's an average of just under 6 minutes per mile, while my winning time in Boston was at an average pace of 4 minutes 54 seconds per mile. This is more the pace that comes naturally to me on those days than something I'm straining to reach. On long runs earlier in a training cycle, I might average closer to 6:15 or 6:30 per mile.

In a good marathon training cycle, I get in several runs of more than 20 miles. The longest I went before winning the Boston Marathon was 26.2 miles. If you start your

WARMUPS AND COOLDOWNS

BEFORE INTERVAL WORKOUTS and tempo runs, I do the same warmup I do before a race, starting with a 3-mile easy run. My warmup routine is detailed in the next chapter. There's no magic to a 3-mile warmup, but you definitely need at least 15 minutes of easy running before running hard to be able to run with your best form and be ready for the first repeat, especially in the cold.

I usually do a 3-mile cooldown jog after the workouts described below, followed by a stretching routine. A few easy miles after a hard session reduces the soreness I'll feel the next day. Try to do at least 10 minutes of jogging after a hard workout. You might feel tired while doing it, but you'll feel better the next day than you would if you immediately went from running hard to doing nothing.

preparation in time and don't hit obstacles, build your long run by a couple of miles each time so that by race day, you've gone longer than 20 miles a few times. On race day, you'll benefit physically and mentally from the experience of running for the amount of time your marathon will take. (I'm talking here primarily to people who will try to run the marathon at faster than their normal training pace. If your marathon goal is more toward the completion end of the spectrum, build up to 22 or 23 miles before race day.)

Combining long runs at a good but not killer pace with tempo runs and intervals gets me ready to race a marathon. I don't do the fast long runs, such as 20 to 25 miles at 10 to 15 seconds per mile slower than mara-

thon pace, that some of my competitors do. That's close to a race effort and probably takes a week to properly recover from. I prefer to keep chipping away consistently.

I also don't do long runs on which I purposely run low on fuel. The idea is that running the last part of your long run in a depleted state will improve your ability to burn fat at a good pace.

"Let me see whether my body will fail" isn't a good goal for a training session. Long runs should leave you pleasantly tired but not exhausted. Always finish long runs feeling like you could run more. Also, finishing long runs like this will probably mean running with worse form, which will increase your injury risk. If anything, I encourage eating a little more than normal the night before a long run so that you have the energy to finish strong.

Long runs are important even if you're not training for a marathon. All runners benefit from improving their endurance; doing so makes all your other runs easier. You don't have to go long every week. Shoot for two or three runs each month that are 25 to 50 percent longer than your other runs.

You shouldn't feel beat up the day after a long run. Take at least 1 recovery day after, but you should be able to run that day without a lot of soreness or stiffness. If you can't do a normal recovery run the day after a long run, then you need to be better about recovery practices the day of the long run. Stretch well, refuel and rehydrate, ice any tender spots, maybe take a walk later in the

NOW THAT I do all my racing on the roads, I don't do hard workouts on the track. Doing interval workouts and tempo runs on a bike path or road better prepares me for my races. My legs get used to the pounding of running hard on asphalt, and I'm not risking aggravating my hip flexor and groin muscles with the constant left turns on the track. Besides, a 15-mile tempo run on the track? No, thank you!

If you like doing workouts on the track, that's fine. If you're mostly a road racer, however, mix things up so that you're not going to the track more than once every 2 weeks. Get used to running hard where you'll be racing. Use the track to get a feel for what various paces feel like, and then apply that information on a bike path or a quiet road.

For tempo runs, I try to mimic the course of my goal race. Before I won the Boston Marathon, I sought out tempo-run courses with lots of ups and downs, with some good uphills in the middle portion and some downhills toward the end. For interval workouts, the focus is on speed and efficiency, so a flatter setting is more important than simulating race courses.

day. If you're okay mechanically but extraordinarily tired, then you need to eat and drink sooner after finishing your long run.

TEMPO RUNS. These runs at a fast but not exhausting effort give you the strength to hold a good pace for a long time. Tempo runs have long been an integral part of my training.

Different runners have different definitions of "tempo" runs. Now that I'm focused on marathons, my tempo runs are a continuous 8 to 15 miles at close to marathon race pace. When I was focusing on shorter races, my tempo runs weren't as long, but they were sometimes run at closer to half-marathon race pace.

You should always feel under control on a tempo run. You're definitely working, but not so hard that you're gasping for breath or at risk of tying up. It's an effort you can sustain for a long time rather than one that has you thinking, "Another few minutes of this and I'm going to have to slow down."

INTERVAL WORKOUTS. Repeats at race pace or faster provide a great stimulus for your cardiovascular system and build your speed and efficiency. The best pace and length of intervals varies widely, depending on what race you're getting ready for.

As a marathoner, I do intervals that are long, such as 2- or 3-mile repeats at about half-marathon race pace, or mile repeats at closer to 10-K race pace. When I was a track racer, a lot of my intervals were faster, more like 5-K race pace on down to mile race pace or even quicker.

There are an infinite number of interval workouts you can do to achieve the same general purpose. For most recreational runners, workouts that total 3 to 4 miles of hard running are best, although as you'll see in the sample schedules that follow starting on page 58, there are times when it makes sense to do more or less than that amount.

ALTITUDE TRAINING HAS BECOME PART OF MY PROGRAM FOR MANY YEARS.

STRIDES. Also known as striders or strideouts, these are fast runs of about 100 meters. The goal is to emphasize quick turnover and accelerating to close to full speed while staying as relaxed as possible. Strides improve your cadence and efficiency at all running paces.

Do strides on a flat, level surface with good footing. They can also be done on the track or a quiet stretch of road or a bike path or well-maintained grass. Doing your first few sessions of strides on a slight downhill will help you get used to accelerating and running with a higher cadence.

I do strides almost every day. I do them as part of my warmup before races, tempo runs, and intervals, and I do them after recovery runs. When I do them before run-

ning hard, I usually do 10. When I do them after recovery runs, I go more by feel. Some days I'll do up to 10, while other days I might do only a few. I usually stop once I feel nice and fluid.

When I focused on shorter races, I also did other workouts to help build my speed, such as 200-meter repeats. As with strides, you want to try to run fast without straining. I would pretend I was a sprinter whose running form I admired, such as four-time Olympic medalist Ato Boldon, while doing these workouts.

RECOVERY RUNS. These are the basic getting-in-the-miles runs that recreational runners most often do. In a well-structured training program leading up to a race, they'll be significantly slower than your harder workouts. I describe my approach to recovery runs at length in Chapter 9.

FARTLEKS. Going fast for a short bit and then returning to easy running over the second half of a run is a great way to introduce quality to your routine. Fartleks are convenient because you can do them anywhere, whenever you feel like pushing the pace.

A variation is adding quick, short bursts to a recovery run. These are 5- to 10-second pickups that you do in the second half, once you're warmed up. They're so short they won't detract from the recovery purpose of the run. If anything, the change of pace will leave you feeling more refreshed.

HILL WORKOUTS. I don't do straightforward hill workouts these days. I incorporate lots of hills into my tempo runs and long runs to prepare for the marathon courses I'll be racing. When I was focused on shorter track and cross-country races, I would convert interval workouts, such as 6 × 800 meters, into hill workouts early in a training cycle.

In 2006, before my first Boston Marathon, I did hill workouts in addition to hilly tempo runs and long runs. On a long hill, I started with 30 seconds hard uphill, and then jogged down 30 seconds for recovery. I increased the hard runs in 15- or 30-second increments, continuing to jog down for the same amount of time as my uphill run, up to 2 minutes. After the 2-minute repeat, I

repeated the sequence in the reverse order (e.g., 2-minute repeat, 90-second repeat, 75-second repeat) and finished with a 30-second repeat.

ALTITUDE TRAINING. Training at altitudes between 4,500 and 9,000 feet has been a very important part of my career. I go to altitude to increase my red blood cell count. Because red blood cells carry oxygen, having a greater red blood cell count means that when I go back to sea level for competition, I breathe easier. For much of my professional career, I lived in Mammoth Lakes, California, which has an altitude of 7,800 feet. I live at sea level in San Diego now, but I return to Mammoth Lakes for an altitude stint just before a marathon.

To get this benefit you need a minimum of 3 weeks at altitude; 4 to 5 weeks is better. I realize that almost no runners with work and family responsibilities can do a month-long altitude training trip. But I want this book to include absolutely everything I do to compete against the best runners in the world.

Sample Training Schedules

There are so many variables that affect what training is best for you. These include your running history, current fitness, goals, available time, susceptibility to injury, and how stressful you find your day-to-day responsibilities. A good training program takes all

TRAINING CYCLE LENGTH

IN MY BUILDUP to winning the Boston Marathon, I used a 9-day training cycle instead of the traditional 7-day cycle most competitive runners use (and that I used for most of my career). I knew that other older elite runners, such as women's marathon world-record holder Paula Radcliffe and Carlos Lopes, who won the 1984 Olympic Marathon at age 37, had switched to a longer cycle as they aged.

The thinking is that you then have more recovery time built in between your key workouts. Consistently doing your long runs, tempo runs, and interval workouts is what's most going to get you ready to race.

My standard week used to be:

- **Sunday: long run**
- **Monday: recovery**
- **Tuesday: interval workout**
- **Wednesday: medium-long run**
- **Thursday: recovery**
- **Friday: tempo run**
- **Saturday: recovery**

On a 9-day cycle, my training looks like this:

- **Day 1: long run**
- **Days 2 and 3: recovery**
- **Day 4: interval workout**
- **Days 5 and 6: recovery**
- **Day 7: tempo run**
- **Days 8 and 9: recovery**

The 9-day cycle left me feeling fresher than I'd been in my past couple of marathon buildups. In fact, sometimes on the 2nd of the recovery days, I felt good enough to push the pace a little, even though I had a hard or long run the next day.

This cycle makes sense for me at this stage of my career. I know that most runners don't have the flexibility I have to do a time-consuming workout any day of the week. You probably have 1 or 2 days a week, and usually always the same days of the week, when you can fit in a long run or a lengthy tempo run.

But I still think there's value in thinking beyond the 7-day training cycle. A lot of runners see something like my old 7-day cycle and try to mimic it in their training. It's one thing to be a 28-year-old professional runner and be able to nail that sort of schedule week after week. It's another to be a 42-year-old with a busy job and other nonrunning responsibilities.

One approach could be to do each key workout—long run, interval workout, and tempo run—once in a 2-week period. If you have the most time on the weekends, that would mean you could do a long run one weekend, then an interval session or tempo run the following weekend, with the other done on a weekday.

Alternatively, you could have a training emphasis to each week. Maybe the first week of the month, you focus on endurance; in addition to a good long run, you get in one or two other decent-length runs. The next week your tempo run becomes the focus, and you maintain your endurance with a shorter long run. Then the next week you focus on your speed with a good interval workout, plus some shorter, faster repeats another day. Put all those together consistently and you'll race well and be able to recover adequately.

that into account and gives you an individualized blueprint for success.

That being the case, what you'll see below are sample blocks of training for each of four popular distances: 5-K, 10-K, half-marathon, and marathon. For each distance, I've first shown how I trained getting ready for an important race, and then put together a short sample of how you might implement my principles in your running.

The training samples are just that, samples, each one 4 weeks long. I don't mean you can adequately prepare for a marathon or even a 5-K in 4 weeks. The samples give a general idea of how various types of workouts might be put together soon before a goal race; specifically, the samples are for a 4-week block that ends with 1 week to go before the race.

Each of the training samples lists the key workouts to do in those 4 weeks. The other days of the week are for recovery runs as needed to reach your typical mileage.

The key workouts aren't assigned to specific days of the week. They should be done on the days that make the most sense in conjunction with the rest of your schedule. The important thing is to allow recovery days between them—don't follow a long run with an interval workout, or a tempo run with a long run.

The workouts are stated in terms of race pace so you can easily figure out what effort level I'm prescribing.

The interval workouts are stated as if you're doing them on a track. You can convert them to off-track workouts, such as on a bike path, by calculating the approximate time for each repeat. For example, the 5-K schedule includes a workout of four 1-mile repeats at close to 5-K race pace. If on the track you would aim to run those in 7 minutes, off the track you could do four 7-minute repeats. In the workouts where a 1-lap recovery jog is called for, substitute a 3-minute jog off the track.

DOS AND DON'TS OF TRAINING

DO include variety in your training program.

DO your hard workouts in settings that simulate race courses.

DO be consistent in how often you run.

DO learn from successful runners' training.

DO keep a training log.

DON'T think that running more will always lead to success.

DON'T run your hard workouts so hard that you're exhausted afterward.

DON'T try to cram too many elements into a training week.

DON'T make drastic sudden increases in mileage or intensity.

DON'T be afraid to take a day off if you feel an injury coming on.

The times given for recovery between intervals are times to be spent jogging, not standing with your hands on your knees. Jogging between repeats helps you recover better.

5-K

Here are 4 weeks of my training soon before I set my 5,000-meter personal record of 13:11.77 on August 5, 2000. These workouts were done at a combination of sea level and altitude.

As it turned out, the race in which I ran 13:11 was a last-minute decision. At that time in my career, it was difficult to get into big track races, and I didn't know I was heading to Europe for the race until 3 days before. As my experience shows, you can sometimes surprise yourself in spur-of-the-moment races, especially if you've been training consistently.

JUNE 19–25

Monday: a.m.—10 miles; p.m.—5 miles

Tuesday: a.m.—3-mile warmup, 3 × 200-meter intervals, 3 × 1-mile intervals, 3-mile cooldown; p.m.—4 miles

Wednesday: 12 miles

Thursday: 3-mile warmup, 8 × 400-meter intervals, 3-mile cooldown

Friday: 3-mile warmup, strides, ½-mile cooldown

Saturday: a.m.—2 miles; p.m.—3-mile warmup, Prefontaine Classic 5,000 meters (10th, 13:48), 2.5-mile cooldown

Sunday: a.m.—10 miles; p.m.—6 miles

JUNE 26–JULY 2

Monday: 10 miles

Tuesday: a.m.—3.5 miles; p.m.—3-mile warmup, 8 × 800-meter intervals, 2 × 200-meter intervals, 3-mile cooldown

Wednesday: 10 miles

Thursday: 3-mile warmup, 3 × (4 × 200-meter intervals), 2.5-mile cooldown

Friday: 2-mile warmup, strides, 1-mile cooldown

Saturday: a.m.—2 miles; p.m.—2.5-mile warmup, Cardinal Invite 5,000 meters (1st, 13:30), 3-mile cooldown

Sunday: 14 miles

JULY 3–9

Monday: 10.5 miles

Tuesday: a.m.—3 miles; p.m.—3-mile warmup, 1-mile interval, 2-mile interval, 1-mile interval, 1-kilometer interval, 800-meter interval, 3 × 150-meter intervals, 3-mile cooldown

Wednesday: 8 miles

Thursday: 3-mile warmup, 10 × 400-meter intervals, 3 × 150-meter intervals, 3-mile cooldown

Friday: 10.5 miles

Saturday: 3-mile warmup, 5-mile tempo run, 2-mile cooldown

Sunday: 8 miles

JULY 10–16

Monday: 3-mile warmup, 800-meter interval, 600-meter interval, 400-meter interval, 1,200-meter interval, 2 × 300-meter intervals, 2 × 150-meter intervals, 2.5-mile cooldown

Tuesday: 6 miles

Wednesday: 2-mile warmup, 3 × (3 × 200-meter intervals), 2-mile cooldown

Thursday: 2-mile warmup, strides, 1-mile cooldown

Friday: a.m.—2 miles; p.m.—3-mile warmup, Olympic Trials 10,000 meters (1st, 28:03), no cooldown except victory lap

Saturday: 3 miles

Sunday: a.m.—7 miles; p.m.—5.5 miles

	KEY WORKOUT #1	KEY WORKOUT #2	KEY WORKOUT #3
WEEK ENDING 4 WEEKS TO RACE DAY	2 × (1 mile, 2 × 1,200 m, 800 m); miles @ 10-K pace with 3:00 recovery; 1,200 m @ 5-K goal pace with 2:30 recovery; 800 m @ mile pace with 2:15 recovery; jog a lap between repeats	2 × (800 m, 600 m, 400 m, 200 m); 800 m @ mile pace, 600 m @ 800 m pace, 400 m @ 600 m pace, 200 m @ 200 m pace; take full recovery between repeats and sets	7–8 mile run @ a little faster than marathon pace
WEEK ENDING 3 WEEKS TO RACE DAY	4 × 1 mile @ close to 5-K pace; 2:00–3:00 recovery between repeats	3 × (4 × 400 m), 400s @ faster than 5-K pace but not all out; 1:15 recovery between 400s; jog a lap between sets	
WEEK ENDING 2 WEEKS TO RACE DAY	1 mile @ a little slower than 5-K pace; 1,200 m @ 5-K pace; 1,000 m @ slightly faster than 5-K pace; 800 m @ faster than 5-K pace; jog a lap between repeats	2-mile run @ 10-K pace	
WEEK ENDING 1 WEEK TO RACE DAY	1 mile, 800 m, 600 m, 400 m; mile @ 10-K pace; all others faster than 5-K race pace but feeling in control; full recovery between repeats; start the next interval when you feel ready	2 × (3 × 300 m) @ 1 mile pace; jog 100 m between intervals; jog a lap between sets	

10-K

Here are 4 weeks of my training soon before I ran 27:13.98 to break the US record for 10,000 meters on May 4, 2001. These workouts were at a combination of sea level and altitude.

APRIL 2–8

Monday: 12 miles

Tuesday: a.m.—10 miles; p.m.—4 miles

Wednesday: 10 miles

Thursday: 10 miles

Friday: 2-mile warmup, 10-mile tempo run, 2-mile cooldown

Saturday: a.m.—10 miles; p.m.—4 miles

Sunday: 16 miles

APRIL 9–15

Monday: 10 miles

Tuesday: a.m.—11 miles; p.m.—4 miles

Wednesday: a.m.—12 miles; p.m.—3 miles

Thursday: a.m.—3-mile warmup, 5 × 1-mile intervals, 3-mile cooldown; p.m.—4 miles

Friday: 12 miles

Saturday: 3-mile warmup, 8-mile tempo run, 3-mile cooldown

Sunday: 20 miles

APRIL 16–22

Monday: 12 miles

Tuesday: 3-mile warmup, 2 × 200-meter intervals, 6 × 1-mile intervals, 1 × 400-meter interval, 3-mile cooldown

Wednesday: 12 miles

Thursday: 3-mile warmup, 3 × (1-kilometer/400-meter/400-meter intervals), 3-mile cooldown

Friday: 12 miles

Saturday: 12 miles, including 5-mile section at tempo-run effort

Sunday: 20 miles

APRIL 23–29

Monday: 12 miles

Tuesday: 3-mile warmup, 5 × ¾-mile intervals, 3.5-mile cooldown

Wednesday: 10 miles

Thursday: 10 miles

Friday: 3-mile warmup, 5.5-mile tempo run, 3-mile cooldown

Saturday: 10.5 miles

Sunday: 3-mile warmup, 2 × (400-meter/400-meter/400-meter/800-meter intervals), 200-meter interval, 400-meter interval, 200-meter interval, 3-mile cooldown

	KEY WORKOUT #1	KEY WORKOUT #2	KEY WORKOUT #3
WEEK ENDING 4 WEEKS TO RACE DAY	6 × 1-mile repeats; first 2 @ marathon pace, second 2 @ slightly slower than 10-K pace, last 2 @ 5-K pace; jog 3:00-4:00 between repeats	3 × (4 × 400 m); 1st set at slower than 10-K pace, 2nd set @ 10-K pace, 3rd set @ 5-K pace; 1:15–1:30 recovery between intervals; jog a lap between sets	
WEEK ENDING 3 WEEKS TO RACE DAY	4–5-mile tempo run @ half-marathon pace or a little faster		
WEEK ENDING 2 WEEKS TO RACE DAY	4–6 1-mile repeats; 1st @ half-marathon pace, remainder @ a few seconds faster than the one before so the last is @ 10-K pace or faster; jog a lap between repeats	3 × (800 m @ 5-K pace/ 600 m @ 3-K pace/400 m @ 1-mile pace); 2:00 recovery after 800 m, 1:30 recovery after 600 m, 1:15 recovery after 400 m; jog a lap between sets	Easy 90-minute run; don't worry about your pace
WEEK ENDING 1 WEEK TO RACE DAY	1 mile, 1,200 m, 800 m, 600 m, 400 m; run each hard but not all out—let loose but don't leave your race on the track; take full recovery between; start the next interval only when you feel ready	6–8 × (3–4 × 200 m); fast but not all out; jog 30–45 seconds between intervals and 1 lap between sets; visualize a sprinter whose form and efficiency you admire	

Half-Marathon

Here are the last 4 weeks of my training before I won the 2009 San Jose Rock 'n' Roll Half Marathon in a personal best of 1:01:00. At this time I was also preparing for the 2009 New York City Marathon, which I won 4 weeks after San Jose. Except for the 3 days before the half-marathon, when I was in San Jose, all of these workouts took place in Mammoth Lakes at altitudes between 7,000 and 9,000 feet.

SEPTEMBER 7–13

Monday: 12 miles

Tuesday: a.m.—3-mile warmup, 8 × 1-mile intervals, 3-mile cooldown; p.m.—5 miles

Wednesday: 20 miles

Thursday: a.m.—10 miles; p.m.—4 miles

Friday: a.m.—3-mile warmup, 15-mile tempo run, 3-mile cooldown; p.m.—5 miles

Saturday: a.m.—10 miles; p.m.—4 miles

Sunday: 26 miles

SEPTEMBER 14–20

Monday: a.m.—10 miles; p.m.—4 miles

Tuesday: a.m.—3-mile warmup, 2 × 1-kilometer intervals, 6 × 1-mile intervals, 2 × 1-kilometer intervals, 3-mile cooldown; p.m.—5 miles

Wednesday: 20 miles

Thursday: a.m.—10 miles; p.m.—4 miles

Friday: a.m.—3-mile warmup, 15-mile tempo run, 3-mile cooldown; p.m.—5 miles

Saturday: a.m.—9 miles; p.m.—7 miles

Sunday: 25 miles

SEPTEMBER 21– 27

Monday: 10 miles

Tuesday: a.m.—3-mile warmup, 8 × 1-kilometer intervals, 4 × 400-meter intervals, 3-mile cooldown; p.m.—4 miles

Wednesday: 15 miles

Thursday: a.m.—10 miles; p.m.—4 miles

Friday: 3-mile warmup, 6-mile tempo run, 3-mile cooldown

Saturday: 10 miles

Sunday: 12 miles

SEPTEMBER 28–OCTOBER 4

Monday: 10 miles

Tuesday: 3-mile warmup, 4 × 400-meter intervals, 2 × 1-kilometer intervals, 4 × 400-meter intervals, 3-mile cooldown

Wednesday: 10.5 miles

Thursday: 7.5 miles

Friday: 5 miles

Saturday: 3-mile warmup, strides, ¾-mile cooldown

Sunday: 3-mile warmup, San Jose Rock 'n' Roll Half Marathon (1st, 1:01:00), 3-mile cooldown

	KEY WORKOUT #1	KEY WORKOUT #2
WEEK ENDING 4 WEEKS TO RACE DAY	5–6 × 1 mile @ half-marathon pace; jog 3:00–4:00 between repeats	8–10-mile tempo run @ between half-marathon and marathon pace
WEEK ENDING 3 WEEKS TO RACE DAY	Last long run: 15–17 miles	3 × (3 × 1,000 m @ 10-K pace); 1:30–2:00 recovery between intervals, 3:00 recovery between sets
WEEK ENDING 2 WEEKS TO RACE DAY	2 × (1 mile @ half-marathon pace, 1,200 m @ 10-K pace, 800 m @ 5-K pace); 3:00 recovery after mile, 2:00 recovery after 1,200 m, 1:30 recovery after 800 m; jog 4:00–5:00 between sets	2 × (4 × 400 m); 1st set @ mile race pace, 2nd set @ 800 m race pace; jog 1:15–1:30 between repeats; jog a lap between sets; focus on relaxed, efficient form
WEEK ENDING 1 WEEK TO RACE DAY	Easy 75-minute run; don't worry about pace	Mile @ half-marathon pace, 1,000 m @ 10-K pace, 800 m @ 5-K pace, 400 m @ mile pace; take as much rest as you need between sets (but not all day!)

Marathon

Here are the last 5 weeks of my training before I won the 2014 Boston Marathon. Except for the 3 days before the marathon, when I was in Boston, all of these workouts took place in Mammoth Lakes at altitudes between 4,000 and 7,800 feet. While tapering, I did a lot fewer ElliptiGO rides than earlier in my preparation for Boston, as I was focusing on running-specific training and conserving energy.

MARCH 18–24

Tuesday: a.m.—10 miles; p.m.—2-hour ElliptiGO ride

Wednesday: 10 miles

Thursday: 3-mile warmup, 11-mile tempo run, 3-mile cooldown

Friday: a.m.—10 miles; p.m.—4 miles

Saturday: a.m.—10.5 miles; p.m.—4 miles

Sunday: 22 miles

Monday: a.m.—10 miles; p.m.—5 miles

MARCH 25–31

Tuesday: a.m.—10 miles; p.m.—4 miles

Wednesday: 3-mile warmup, 6 × 1-mile intervals, 2 × ¼-mile intervals, 5-mile cooldown

Thursday: 16 miles

Friday: a.m.—10 miles; p.m.—4 miles

Saturday: a.m.—3-mile warmup, 12-mile tempo run, 3-mile cooldown; p.m.—5-miles

Sunday: a.m.—12 miles; p.m.—4 miles

Monday: 12 miles

APRIL 1–7

Tuesday: 26 miles

Wednesday: 12 miles

Thursday: 12 miles

Friday: a.m.—3-mile warmup, 10-mile tempo run, 3-mile cooldown; p.m.—4 miles

Saturday: a.m.—10 miles; p.m.—4 miles

Sunday: a.m.—10 miles; p.m.—5 miles

Monday: 20 miles

APRIL 8–14

Tuesday: 12.5 miles

Wednesday: 12 miles

Thursday: Day off. My right quad felt sore and weak. I could have run—and would have in my youth—but by then knew that doing so on that day could set me back. I stayed focused on the big goal of winning the Boston Marathon and did an hour ride on a stationary bike and got therapy. This is a good example of knowing your body and remaining flexible with your training program instead of being tied to a set routine.

Friday: 3-mile warmup, 6-mile tempo run, 3-mile cooldown

Saturday: 10 miles

Sunday: 12.5 miles

Monday: 3-mile warmup, 2 × ¼-mile intervals, 2 × 1-kilometer intervals, 2 × 1-mile intervals, 2 × ½-mile intervals, 2 × ¼-mile intervals, 4-mile cooldown

APRIL 15–21

Tuesday: 13 miles

Wednesday: 10 miles

Thursday: 3-mile warmup, 4 × 200-meter intervals, 4 × 400-meter intervals, 4 × 300-meter intervals, 2 × 200-meter intervals, 4-mile cooldown

Friday: 4 miles

Saturday: 5 miles

Sunday: 3-mile warmup, strides, ¾-mile cooldown

Monday: 2-mile warmup, stretching and drills, then a 5-minute run and 8 x100-meter strides, Boston Marathon, 1st place, 2:08:37

	KEY WORKOUT #1	KEY WORKOUT #2	KEY WORKOUT #3
WEEK ENDING 4 WEEKS TO RACE DAY	5–6 × 1 mile @ 10–15 seconds per mile faster than marathon pace; 2:30–3:00 recovery between repeats		10–12-mile tempo run at marathon pace
WEEK ENDING 3 WEEKS TO RACE DAY	Last long run: 21–23 miles		2 × (1 mile @ half-marathon pace, 1,000 m @ 10-K pace, 800 m @ 5-K pace, 400 m @ mile pace); 3:00 recovery after mile, 2:00 after 1,200 m, 1:30 after 800 m, 1:15 after 400 m; jog 4:00 between sets
WEEK ENDING 2 WEEKS TO RACE DAY	15–18-mile run		8-mile tempo run, about 10–15 seconds per mile faster than marathon pace
WEEK ENDING 1 WEEK TO RACE DAY	75 minutes easy; don't worry about pace	60 minutes easy; don't worry about pace	45 minutes with 8 × 100 m strides at the end

Race like Meb

How to be your best physically and mentally on race day

RACING IS like graduation day. It's the opportunity to put all your hard work toward giving 100 percent, physically and mentally. Like a lot of runners, I like to train, but I love to race.

In this chapter I'll describe what I do soon before and during a race to be my best. We'll look at warming up and otherwise getting ready for the start, race nutrition, and, perhaps most important, the psychological side of racing.

Before the Race

I AM proof that you can race well despite poor sleep the night before a race. I'm usually so keyed up before a goal race that I can't sleep soundly. Before I won the Boston Marathon, I was up probably every hour after midnight. As I'll describe in this chapter's nutrition section, I've learned to use that reality to my advantage. So take it from me: Don't stress out if you don't sleep well the night before a race. Focus on getting good sleep in the week heading into the race.

Before races that aren't my main focus of the season, I sometimes sleep more soundly. How soon I get up before the race depends on how far I am from the start. The setup in Houston, where I won the 2012 Olympic Marathon Trials and 2009 and 2014 national half-marathon championships, is ideal—the race hotel overlooks the start/finish area. In a situation like that, assuming I haven't been up all night, I'll wake up about 2 hours before race time. You don't need to eat much (some runners don't need anything) before shorter races, so you don't have to build in time for digestion like you do before a marathon. No matter how close you live to a race, get up at least 2 hours before start time so you don't have to rush and are fully awake when it's time to run hard.

Before I leave for the start, I do about 10 minutes of stretching and a few other exercises, including using a foam roller.

I like to be at the race site 75 minutes before the start. Ideally, I start warming up an hour before the start. This isn't always possible at big races because of logistics. Or sometimes things happen and your schedule gets thrown off. Have a warmup routine that you know works for you, but don't get too tied to it in case surprises pop up. You don't want to go to the start thinking, "There's no way I can race well today because I had to alter my warmup."

The first major part of my warmup routine is a 3-mile jog. I usually go that far for all races, even marathons. That's right—I did a 3-mile warmup before I won the Boston Marathon. That's the warmup run I've become used to over nearly 20 years. I don't worry that it's going to cause me to hit the wall during the marathon. Between my training and prerace and race-day nutrition, I'm confident I'll have enough fuel to get me to the finish.

I start my warmup jog nice and slow. How slow varies by the day, but it's usually no faster than about 8 minutes per mile for the first few minutes. To put that in perspective, that's about 3 minutes per mile slower than my marathon pace and 3½ minutes slower than my 10-K pace. Ease into it and let your body gradually get loose and warm. I pick up the pace throughout my warmup, but only as doing so feels natural. It's much more "Oh, I'm running faster at the same effort" than "Now that I've run a mile and a half, I need to speed up." By the end I'm running at a steady, comfortable pace, more like 1 to 1½ minutes per mile slower than race pace.

Bear in mind that my 3-mile warmup takes just over 20 minutes. If you're aiming to run the race significantly faster than you train, I think you should get in at least 15 to 20 minutes of easy running before. If you're worried about hitting the wall in a marathon, keep it at for more like 10 minutes. Have the confidence from your training that a good warmup isn't going to drain you. Because I do the same warmup before my interval workouts and tempo runs, my race-day routine is familiar and comforting.

This is one major difference I've noticed between elites and many recreational runners—we warm up more aggressively, so that we're truly ready to run hard right from the gun. Think about how much better you usually feel 3 miles into a run or on the second or third repeat of an interval workout. Aim to start races with that same

WHEN NOT TO START A RACE

INJURIES HAPPEN TO all of us. When you're in the middle of trying to get over an injury, races are out of the question. Your priority is to get healthy.

Sometimes at the time of an important race, you're over the injury and back to good training, but you're short on fitness. That's why I didn't run the 2008 New York City and 2013 Boston Marathons. I felt I was in good shape, but not good enough to race a marathon against some of the best runners in the world. It wasn't worth it to me to produce a so-so effort and then have to go through the whole cycle of recovery and starting back up. I told myself, "Stay healthy and use this as motivation for next year." In both cases, I won the race the following year in a personal best.

It's always going to be a judgment call in these situations. I would say if you're at 75 percent or less of the fitness you want for a race, reconsider. Do like I did—stay healthy and motivated for when you can be at your best.

feeling of all cylinders firing. Even if your goal is to finish a half-marathon or marathon without regard to time, jog a few minutes before the start. You'll feel better in the early miles and won't be so nervous waiting to find out how you're going to feel running that day.

The main exception concerning my warmup jog is if it's really hot. For example, before I won the silver medal at the 2004 Olympic Marathon in Athens, I jogged only a mile. It was close to 90°F when we started. It didn't take much for my muscles to feel warm and loose. Also, I was pretty sure the race would start slowly in such heat, so I could ease into race pace more so than is usually possible.

Sometimes I split my warmup jog in two. I most often do this if it's really cold and I want to try to stay warm before the start. I've also done this if I realize the start is going to be delayed. So I might run a mile and a half, then do some of the stretching and drills I'll describe later in this chapter, then run another mile and a half, then do my prerace strides (also described later).

After my warmup jog, it's time to stretch. I do about 10 minutes of what's called active isolated stretching, which some people call rope stretching. This is a dynamic way of stretching in which you stretch one muscle by using its opposing muscle to produce a movement; you use the rope to guide the movement and to extend the stretch at the end of the motion.

SUNGLASSES ON RACE DAY

I USUALLY WEAR sunglasses in a race if it's a sunny day. This is not because of the sun but to help keep my head at the right level.

When you get tired, it's natural to put your head down. As I discussed in Chapter 2, not holding your head level can throw off your form, which in a race situation will just make you feel that much more tired.

If you're wearing sunglasses when you lower your head, they'll start to slide down your nose. When that happens, it's a cue to return your head to a level position, looking 20 to 30 meters down the road.

For example, to stretch your hamstrings, you lie on your back and raise your leg while contracting your quadriceps, which are the opposing muscles to the hamstrings. The full routine I do before a race, and a longer explanation of active isolated stretching, are described in Chapter 7.

As an invited runner, I usually have access to a reserved area near the start to use as the base for my warmup. That's where I stretch. At a lot of races your base will be the vehicle you traveled to the race in. Bring a towel or yoga mat to put on the ground so that you can comfortably stretch after your warmup jog. Having a base that's a short jog from the start isn't always possible, especially at big races. Again, be open to breaks in your routine and the need to improvise. For example, you can achieve many of the results of active isolated stretching with leg swings and other dynamic movements.

After I'm done stretching, I put Vaseline on my toes, the bottoms of my feet, and my private parts and under my arms to reduce chafing. (I still usually get some during a marathon.) I change into my racing shoes and fresh socks. Even if you don't wear different shoes to race in, put on a dry pair of socks after your warmup jog to reduce your risk of blistering. Throughout the time I'm stretching and getting dressed to race, I sip water or an electrolyte drink.

By this point, my muscles are warm and loose, and it's time to do drills to further prepare my body to perform at its highest level. As described in Chapter 2, these drills take

DEALING WITH DELAYED STARTS

BIG RACES LIKE the Boston and New York City Marathons usually go off like clockwork. That makes it easy to plan your warmup. But sometimes weather or a logistical issue can mean a long time between ending your warmup jog and the start. You need to be ready for surprises like this so you don't panic and think your chance of having a good race has been ruined.

My worst experience with this was at the 2003 World Championships. American sprinter Jon Drummond was disqualified from the quarterfinals of the 100-meter dash for a false start. He disputed the ruling and refused to leave the track. At one point he laid down on the track. The incident wound up delaying the rest of the evening's events, including my 10,000-meter race, by almost an hour. We 10-K runners had to strike a balance—we needed to stay loose and warmed up, but we didn't know how long the meet was going to be held up, and we couldn't just keep jogging and doing strides forever.

One thing I did was to lie on my back and put my feet up to help keep good blood circulation going. If I faced that situation again, I'd do dynamic stretches, such as leg swings and squats, to keep my muscles warm.

This is similar to what a lot of recreational runners face before the really big road races. You're often made to get in your start corral 20 or more minutes before the start. If you know that's going to be the case, then time your warmup jog so that you finish it soon before you have to line up. Also do some strides then, because you probably won't have clear running room until after the race starts. Bring water or an electrolyte drink with you. Once you're in your corral, do the bulk of your stretching there. Focus on movements like arm swings, squats, marching, and Quick Feet that you can do in close quarters. If you can, stay by the side of the corral, where the fencing is, and do some leg swings. This should keep your muscles warm, your heart rate elevated, and your blood circulating rather than pooling in your feet.

me through a greater range of motion than running does. They also help prime my central nervous system, so that I have more efficient communication between my brain and my muscles. Before a race, the drills I focus on are mostly variations of skips and lunges. I also do some drills that involve lateral movement. This is not only to make sure all the small stabilizing muscles of the hips and glutes are engaged but also to help me quickly move sideways if necessary during the crowded first few miles. (See Chapter 2 for full descriptions of the running form drills I do.)

The last part of my warmup is strides, which are runs of about 100 meters in which I accelerate to about 5-K race pace. (For more about strides, see Chapter 3, Train like Meb.) Before a short race like a 10-K, I'll do 10 to 12 strides. I never force the pace on these. Build into each one, and let the speed come out naturally as you get better warmed up. If there's room before a shorter race, I'll do 1 or 2 fewer strides and finish with about 200 meters at race pace. Before a marathon, when I don't need to be as ready to run hard right from the start, I usually do 8 to 10 strides.

Strides are the final step in preparing my body to handle race pace right from the

A GOOD WARMUP PREPARES YOU TO RUN FAST WITH GOOD FORM.

start. Again, think about how much better you usually feel on the second or third repeat of an interval workout than the first. By then your cardiovascular system is fully primed to work at max capacity, whereas during your first repeat the body is sort of in a state of shock. The same principle applies to racing—you want the start to be something your body is completely ready for.

Strides also help to make sure that I'm ready mechanically to handle the first few minutes of the race without strain. The starts of big races are always so chaotic, with

people sprinting off the line and thousands of people behind me. My biggest concern is whether I'm going to get knocked over. I usually start out faster than race pace to get clear running room, then settle in once I see that I have the room around me to run without fear of falling.

Having begun some races farther back in the pack, I know how challenging those starts can be. You're crowded, crowded, crowded, then all of a sudden open road appears and people take off like crazy. Being fully warmed up, including doing strides, will prepare you to quickly transition to race pace in those situations.

That's the physical part of my warmup. I'm also preparing mentally throughout that time. I usually do my warmup jog by myself while listening to music on my Meb-edition Sony Walkman, a wireless MP3 player. The music I listen to is mostly fast-tempo, pump-up songs by artists like James Brown, Michael Jackson, and Eminem. (In case you're wondering, yes, I sometimes listen to "Eye of the Tiger" by Survivor.) I visualize various race scenarios, what it's going to feel like, and whom I'm going to watch out for. I run through my goals for the day. (See later in this chapter for my approach to race-day goal setting.)

On the start line, I take time to calm myself and just be thankful I'm there. One of the things I was thinking before the 2014 Boston Marathon was "Last year I wasn't healthy and couldn't run here. Now I'm healthy. I'm thankful to get to run this race, and I hope to give my best."

Right before the gun goes off, I'm in meditation mode. I pray internally as the national anthem is sung, thinking about what these words mean and how special it is to be there on that day. I think about how fortunate we are to be able-bodied and to have the opportunity to test ourselves in this way. I think, "May the best man or woman win today." I hope I'm the most prepared one, but if somebody has worked harder than me, then they deserve to win. That's my mentality going into a race.

VISUALIZING RACES DURING TRAINING

THINK ABOUT YOUR goal race on training runs. Picture yourself on the course, running well and finishing strong. If you're unfamiliar with the course, find an online guide to help you visualize running on it.

For example, before the New York City Marathon, I might be approaching a spot on one of my training loops where I know there's a couple of turns and an incline. I'll tell myself, "Okay, think about New York. You're in Central Park. It's the toughest part of the race. Run up and over the hill. Stay light. Stay tall." Or I'll be doing a tempo run, and toward the end I'll will myself, "It's the last 2 miles of the race. Focus on your technique. Your arm swing is good. Quick feet. Relax your shoulders."

I also visualize races when I run with others. I might tuck in to the back of a group and think, "Okay, here we are, the lead pack running up First Avenue in Manhattan during New York. Someone's going to make a move. Be ready."

I start doing this a few months before a marathon. I'd rather have run through all the scenarios in my head than suddenly start thinking about the race the week before. Constantly remind your body what it's getting ready for so that anything that can happen on race day already feels familiar.

Race Nutrition

THE NEXT chapter, Eat like Meb, is all about my day-to-day diet. One of the points I make in that chapter is that, as with training, you should learn from others without thinking you need to copy them. Take others' advice and see how well it works for you.

So in terms of what to eat and drink soon before and during a race, I'm going to describe the system I've developed over time. If you like some of these ideas, test them to see if they should become part of your race routine.

EATING AND DRINKING THE DAY BEFORE A NONMARATHON RACE. Before something like a 10-K or half-marathon, I try to stick as closely as possible to my normal diet. Lunch might be a turkey sandwich with lettuce and tomato, but no mayonnaise, on whole wheat bread.

Throughout the day before a race, I snack on fruits. As with what I have for lunch, this is what I do at home on a normal day.

What I have for dinner depends on the situation I find myself in, since I'm almost always at a hotel or staying at a host family's house. If I have a choice, I'll have something nutritious but bland, such as chicken with rice and vegetables. I'd rather not have a heavy meal or one with a lot of fiber or spices. Any of those could come back to haunt me on race morning.

I don't think you should go overboard with carbohydrates the night before a short race. Running out of fuel isn't a risk in a 10-K or even a half-marathon.

I also don't think you should radically change what or how much you drink the day before a race. After all, good hydration habits are part of good training. People might see me walking around with a water bottle the day before a race and think, "Oh, I should do like Meb and drink lots and lots of water before tomorrow." But the thing is, I always walk around with a water bottle.

Judge your hydration status by the color of your urine. If it's beige or a little bit gold, like light cream, then you're fine. That shows that what you've consumed is still in your system. If it's as pale as water, you've hydrated so much that you've washed away nutrients, particularly sodium. You want to be making regular but not constant visits to the restroom.

EATING AND DRINKING THE DAY BEFORE A MARATHON. Even the day before a marathon, I mostly stick to my normal diet. The body thrives on routine. Why suddenly start eating differently just before you're going to ask your body to perform at its max?

For lunch I might have pasta, which isn't something I often do at home, if I can easily get to a good restaurant. But if not, then I'll have a turkey sandwich. I'll snack on fruits during the afternoon. Again, that's nothing different from what I would do at home.

Having spent part of my childhood in

Italy, I'm partial to eating pasta the night before a marathon. I love to have spaghetti with meatballs. If not, any kind of pasta or even rice with a simple sauce is fine.

I don't agree with the idea that you should gorge yourself the night before a marathon. That one meal isn't going to be what determines whether you run strong to the finish. Eating too much could lead to stomach issues or pit stops the next morning, as well as interfere with your sleep. You should feel full but not bloated after your dinner the night before a marathon.

EATING AND DRINKING THE MORNING OF A NONMARATHON RACE. I like a little something in my stomach before a 10-K or half-marathon, such as a piece of toast or half a bagel with honey and/or nut butter. I might have this 2 hours or more before the start, depending on when I get up.

Bear in mind that I'm used to eating this amount of food an hour or so before most of my morning runs. Some runners prefer to race on an empty stomach. I certainly don't advise having a bagel soon before a short race if you usually run early in the morning without eating anything. As always, experiment to see what works best for you.

EATING AND DRINKING THE MORNING OF A MARATHON. Here's where I've learned to turn what could be a negative—my usual fitful sleep the night before a marathon—to my advantage.

The day before the marathon, I gather my supplies for overnight eating. On the nightstand next to the bed, I line up a bottle of sports drink, a banana, and two or three whole wheat bread or bagel sandwiches with almond butter and/or honey. When, inevitably, I can't sleep and I look at the clock and it says 1:30 or 1:45, I think, "You know what? I'm just going to eat." Over the next few hours I eat a decent number of calories. By the time I've eaten my sandwiches, I've probably taken in as many calories as the people who stuffed themselves at the prerace pasta party. But by eating smaller amounts more frequently, I'm not making my digestive system work overtime, and my blood sugar stays at a more constant level.

Another advantage of this system: When most of my competitors sit down for their prerace breakfast at 5:00 or 6:00 a.m., they're thinking, "How much should I eat? I haven't eaten since last night. I feel hungry. I know I need to fuel up. But if I eat too much, I'm going to have an upset stomach during the race. I better have just a banana and half a bagel." In contrast, at that time I'm thinking, "I'm already fueled. I'll just have a little oatmeal or a piece of toast and maybe an egg to top off the tank." (If I feel I've eaten enough, I stay in my room and stretch.)

I continue to sip sports drink in the few hours before the start. I aim to have taken in 16 to 20 ounces that morning before I start my warmup routine. I listen to my body to see if I need anything else to eat. If I start to feel hungry, I'll have half or all of a banana

FOOLING YOUR BRAIN WITH SPORTS DRINK

SOMETIMES DURING A race I'll grab some sports drink, swish a little bit around in my mouth, and then spit it out. Recent research has found that, when you're working hard, doing this sends a signal to your brain that more sugar is on the way. In studies where people have wet their mouths with sports drink but not swallowed it, their rating of perceived exertion is lower (that is, a given pace feels a little easier) and their time to exhaustion is greater (they can maintain a given pace for longer).

It's a fascinating illustration of just how much of a mind game racing can be.

I most often do this swish-and-spit technique, or maybe just take a couple of sips, in the second half of a marathon, when my stomach can be more unsettled than earlier in the race. Sometimes I do it as late as the 40-kilometer mark, when I have only about 6 minutes of running left. I think about getting that last drink and how it will help me get to the finish strong. Maybe it's a placebo effect, but so what? At that point I'll take any help I can get.

or an energy gel (PowerGel, made by Power-Bar, one of my sponsors).

Soon before a marathon, you don't want to wait to eat until you're hungry. It's like waiting to get hydrated. By the time you feel you need something, you've already hampered your performance.

NUTRITION DURING THE RACE. During shorter races, I almost never drink anything but water. So what I'm about to describe pertains to marathons.

The typical setup for the professional field is that there are fluid stations every 5 kilometers. We get to have a bottle of the fluid of our choice at those aid stations.

What's in my bottle depends on where the aid station is on the course. My basic bottles contain a sports drink with carbohydrates and electrolytes. My bottles at the 15-kilometer, 20-kilometer, 25-kilometer, and 30-kilometer aid stations contain sports drink mixed with a caffeinated PowerGel.

I try to get my bottle at every aid station. Unless there are important moves being made by someone in the pack, I carry my bottle for a while and try to get in 6 to 8 ounces. I take just a few sips at a time rather than chugging it down. I put the drink in my mouth, let it come to my throat, and then swallow it down.

I keep drinking at every aid station, even the one at 40 kilometers. (See "Fooling Your Brain with Sports Drink.")

I practice drinking on my long runs and tempo runs. I'm fortunate to usually have someone accompanying me on a bike for these workouts. I give them two bottles. As in the marathon, one has sports drink in it, and the other has sports drink mixed with a caffeinated gel. (I learned that trick from my fellow Olympic marathoner Ryan Hall. It sure beats carrying the gels and having them freeze or cutting your lip trying to open them on the run.) On long runs, I have the bottle with the dissolved gel at 12, 15, and 21 miles.

RACE LIKE MEB **77**

The overwhelming majority of runners don't get to put bottles out on race courses. But I think there are still some important ideas here anyone can make use of.

First, learn to drink, and drink a fair amount, while running fast. Practice drinking on at least every long run so that you learn how to swallow without choking and how to keep breathing normally. Also practice running with your drink for a long time so that doing so feels normal on race day.

Second, practice with the drink you'll be using during the marathon. Find out what the race will have out on the course. Give it at least a few tries before deciding whether it agrees with you. If it doesn't, carry your own during long races.

Third, start drinking early in the race, and keep at it throughout. Don't wait until you feel thirsty—by then, your performance has decreased significantly.

Finally, see if it will be possible for someone to hand you a bottle once or twice during the race. This will allow an opportunity to really get some fluid down, given how much easier it is to drink from a bottle than a paper cup. And you'll be able to try my gel-dissolved-in-sports-drink concoction.

The Key to Racing: Mental Strength and Flexibility

ONCE THE gun goes off, racing is 90 percent mental and 10 percent physical.

I don't mean that anyone can simply will themselves to win a race or set a personal best. Ultimately, your range of possible results depends on how fit you are that day. What I mean is that, once you start the race, how close you come to getting the most out of that fitness is largely based on making good decisions and staying strong mentally.

Races are inherently challenging. Look at them as opportunities to do the best you're capable of. Not tomorrow, not next week or next month, but today. Make a wise and good decision to maximize your training.

You can help yourself even before the start by staying relaxed mentally. Some runners on the start line look absolutely terrified. I've never been that bad, but I used to be much more nervous on the start line than I am now. I used to worry, "How am I going to do? What am I going to do? Who's at my right? Who's at my left? What should I be doing right now?"

WHEN NOT TO FINISH A RACE

I'VE DROPPED OUT of three races as a professional runner. The first was the 10,000-meter final at the 2005 World Championships in Helsinki. I stopped after 5 kilometers. I simply couldn't run any farther without excruciating pain. I later learned I had a longitudinal tear 2 centimeters wide and 11 centimeters long in my right quadriceps.

The second DNF was at the San Jose Rock 'n' Roll Half Marathon in 2006. I was one of the founders of the race and was aiming for the American record. But I was also training through the race, rather than tapering for it, and had run 120 miles in the previous week. I was well on pace to get the record until I got a cramp in my right hamstring. I had to stop and get a ride to the finish from a cop on a motorcycle.

My third dropout was at the 2007 London Marathon. The month before I had developed a golf-ball-size blister on my left foot that had to be drained. When I could resume running, I was compensating for it and wound up irritating my right Achilles, which got increasingly worse in London. I dropped out after about 16 miles because I didn't want to risk a much more serious injury by running hard in such a compromised state for another 10 miles.

In each of those instances, my body was telling me loud and clear that I had no business trying to race. To me, that's the trigger for dropping out—if an injury significantly alters my form and continuing to run on it is going to make things that much worse or, as in Helsinki, running has become impossible.

Like so many things in running, it's a judgment call. At the 2013 New York City Marathon, I ran in the lead pack during the first two-thirds of the race. Then my calves started cramping. I spent the rest of the race walking, jogging, and running as my calves would allow. I finished in 2:23:47, the slowest marathon of my career. To me, this was a different situation than Helsinki and London—my calves were cramping, not tearing. I was pretty sure it was just a really bad day at the office, not a serious injury that would lead to long-term damage if I continued to run.

If you're having a bad day and not running up to your potential but aren't hurt, finish the race. You'll like yourself so much more later in the day than if you drop out. Use the bad race as a learning opportunity, figure out what you need to do differently, and come back that much more ready next time.

With experience I've become much more at ease before the start. Sure, I'm anxious. But I'm also excited—the moment I've been working so hard toward the last several months is finally here! I've also become very comfortable doing prerace interviews and talking with other runners. I try to keep it a fun environment and not use up any of the mental energy I'll need during the race.

One of the most important decisions in a race comes in the first mile. Do you have the wisdom and maturity to go out at the right pace, or do you get caught up in the emotional rush of a race and start out at a pace that you can't sustain to the finish?

Once you're under way at a reasonable pace, the mind games begin. The way to win the mind games—and do the best you can on that day—is to have a plan.

When I say "a plan," I mean a full set of goals, from A to Z. Goal A is the ultimate you hope to achieve that day. Goal B is your first backup; it's still a great result. Each subsequent goal is a little further away from goal A. Each one should be something that will give you focus and determination if it becomes obvious your higher goals aren't possible that day.

For me, goal A is usually to win. For you, it might be to set a personal best or, if it's your first time doing a race of that distance, to get to the finish line. My goal B is usually to get on the podium (finish among the top three). Yours might be to run the fastest you have for the distance in the last 5 years. My goal C might be to be the top American. Yours might be your fastest time ever on the course you're running. And so on down through several more possible outcomes.

This approach will motivate you to keep fighting to the finish. Consider the alternative: You say, "Today my only goal is to set a personal best." But then by halfway your splits tell you it's not going to happen. So what now? Just as you're entering the hardest part of the race, you're adrift. When that little voice asks, "Why am I doing this?" there's no good response. You lose focus and drive and wind up running much slower than you're capable of. Then you spend the rest of the day disgusted with yourself.

In contrast, if you had a goal B of running the fastest you have in the last 5 years, you'd stay engaged. You'd keep pushing because when that little voice asks, "Why am I doing this?" you can say, "Because seeing this through to the end is going to mean I'll cover this distance faster than I have for

5 years. And that's something to be proud of." You finish strong, not too far off your personal best, congratulate yourself on a good job, and have motivation to keep training hard for another attempt at your personal best.

The idea here is to find the positive spin on whatever the current situation is as a way to keep yourself motivated. When you're coming up with your goals for a race, be ready for any situation. Hope for the best, plan for the worst; that's part of racing. During the race, constantly evaluate how it's going, and be flexible in deciding what your goal is given how the day is playing out.

This in no way means to start lowering your sights as soon as things aren't going perfectly. I fight for each of my goals as long as possible if there's even a slight chance I might achieve it. And after the race, I'm honest with myself about how close I ran to my potential on that day.

As I've mentioned, I'm not the most talented guy. I've been lapped in 10,000-meter races on the track. During my first Olympics, in Sydney in 2000, in the second half of the race I could see the leaders on the other side of the track. I could have thought, "How embarrassing. The whole world is watching. I'm so far behind, so what does it matter where I finish?" Instead, as events played out, I shifted my goal to being the first American finisher. I concentrated on trying to beat the other American in the race, Abdi Abdirahman. I was thinking, "If he's going to beat me, he's going to have to earn it." As it turned out, Abdi finished 10th and I was 12th. But we both set personal bests.

Then, when I did my post-race assessment, I thought, "Okay, I've had the flu. I was a little weak coming into the race. So there's room for improvement." In my next track 10,000, I lowered my personal best by 40 seconds and set an American record that lasted for 9 years. Having flexible goals allowed me to get the best out of myself that night in Sydney and helped set the stage for an even better performance the next time I tackled the distance.

Another example of how this mental approach has helped me race my best on any given day is the 2012 Olympic Marathon in London. I finished fourth at age 37, 8 years after my Olympic silver medal, even though the race was a struggle almost the whole way.

I'd had a couple of injuries during my buildup and was a few weeks away from peak fitness. I figured the race would start fast, so my race plan was to let the leaders go, run in the chase pack, and then pick off as many of the frontrunners as possible in the later miles.

At the Olympics, as at big marathons like Boston and New York City, there are aid stations every 5 kilometers. We elites can put bottles of our preferred drinks, the ones we train with, at each aid station. At one of the early aid stations in London, I was given the bottle that was supposed to go to one of my teammates, Ryan Hall. I didn't know what was in his bottle and didn't want to drink from it. Ryan, who would drop out after about 10 miles with a hamstring injury, was already well back. I had to slow to let him catch up, in the hope he had my bottle. He didn't. I gave him his, he drank some, then told me to finish it off. I did because it was already hot and I knew I needed to drink.

Ryan's drink didn't settle well in my stomach. I started cramping and lost contact with the second pack. Also, the cobblestones on the course were giving me a blister on my left foot, which I've had problems with since 2007. At one point I fell back to 21st place. Things were going from bad to worse.

For a moment, I thought, "Drop out. I've won New York. I have an Olympic silver medal. I don't want to do further damage to the foot and then have to miss New York City in 3 months. Call it a day." But then I thought, "No, this is the situation that I'm in, and I'm going to make the best of it."

I thought back to when I won the Olympic Marathon Trials in January of that year. I had said, "We're sending our best team, and I hope we can represent our country very well." Dropping out wasn't an option. So I told myself, "You're going to get to the finish line no matter what, no matter how many people pass you."

I concentrated. I prayed. I asked for the strength to get back up to the second group. When I caught the second group, I told

WINNING THE 2009 NEW YORK CITY MARATHON IN A USA JERSEY IS ONE OF MY CAREER HIGHLIGHTS.

myself, "If I can beat one person in this group, I'd be happy with that." I started feeling a little better. I thought, "Maybe I can beat two of them."

As others started falling out of our pack, I gained mental strength. I had been close to dropping out but was now moving up the leaderboard. By the 30-kilometer mark, I was in 10th. A Japanese runner, Kentaro Nakamoto, started surging. I latched on to him and hoped to be pulled along. I was hurting so bad, but I told myself, "Just hang on, then pass him at the end." Instead of doing like I usually do and following the line on the road indicating the shortest route, I hung on to Nakamoto for dear life.

At 37 kilometers, with just more than 3 miles to run, I saw my longtime coach, Bob Larsen, hold out six fingers. I'd lost count. I didn't know if it meant I was in sixth place or Nakamoto was in sixth place. This would have been a good place to clarify or take time-out to consult with a coach, as in other sports, but in a marathon you can consult only yourself. Then I saw a green jersey up ahead. I started doing the math in my head: "If I'm in sixth, then the green jersey is in fourth. Who knows, maybe one of the medalists will fail a drug test and be stripped of his medal. If I can catch the green jersey, there's a slight chance I could be a medalist again!"

People often ask if I pay attention to the crowd during races. I sure do! I love when they scream my name or "Go, USA!" In this race, about 1 kilometer from the finish, I heard someone yell my name and that I could catch the next guy. It turned out to be a fellow American, Phil Racht of Atlanta, who came to watch me run.

I passed the runner in the green jersey, two-time New York City Marathon champion Marílson Gomes dos Santos, with 500 meters to go. I was so excited about how I'd gone from almost dropping out to finishing fourth that as I approached the finish line and saw a spectator with an American flag, I grabbed it and ran with it above my head to the finish. Maybe only the winner is supposed to do this. But I felt like I'd had a huge personal victory, thanks to constant internal communication and goal assessment as the race unfolded.

Not every race you run is going to be a home run. But every race, good or bad, can be a learning experience. Do an assessment after each race. Wait at least until later that day, when the emotions of the moment have lessened. Ask yourself, "Did I give 100 percent? Did I run up to my ability on that day?" If so, hold your head high. What more could you ask of yourself?

We often learn the most when things don't go well. After a not-so-great race, figure out what was missing. Were you a few weeks short on training? Did you go out too fast? Did you have a mental lapse two-thirds of the way into the race? Be honest but not too hard on yourself. Instead, look at the race as a springboard to a better performance next time. There's always room for improvement.

DOS AND DON'TS OF RACING

DO a full warmup before racing, even for long races.

DO practice drinking on the run so that doing so feels normal in races.

DO visualize upcoming races in training.

DO have several goals for each race.

DO an evaluation after every race to find areas for improvement.

DON'T worry about bad sleep the night before a race.

DON'T panic if your prerace routine gets thrown off.

DON'T radically change your diet the day before a race.

DON'T drop out of a race unless you're injured.

DON'T beat yourself up after a bad race.

Eat like Meb

The best daily diet to fuel your running

I GET asked, "What do you eat?" at least as often as I'm asked, "How do you train?" A lot of people seem to think I have special nutrition secrets that make me so fast. Others think more or less the opposite— that as someone running more than 100 miles a week, I eat whatever I want whenever I want.

The truth is between those two extremes. In this chapter I'll give you an overview of my day-to-day diet and how it helps my running. (What to eat and drink soon before and during a race was covered in the previous chapter, Race like Meb.) I'll also share my advice for watching your weight as a runner, which is something I work on more than you might think a champion marathoner would.

What's a Good Running Diet?

MY CRITERIA for a good running diet are simple.

• **A good running diet fuels your training but doesn't interfere with it.**

• **A good running diet keeps you healthy.**

• **A good running diet helps you maintain a good running weight.**

RUNNING AND VEGETARIANISM

I'VE NEVER CONSIDERED trying to be a vegetarian. I think for an elite athlete, it's hard to be one and perform at your absolute best. Especially in terms of iron, which helps build the red blood cells that carry oxygen, I want to make sure I'm meeting 100 percent of my needs. Also, eating meat is part of my Eritrean upbringing.

Of course, there are many successful endurance athletes who are vegetarians. They are serious about nutrition and get high-quality protein from sources such as tofu, beans, and, for those who eat them, eggs. I certainly have admiration for people who are vegetarians because they think it's a more humane way to eat. I might try being one when I'm no longer competing at the highest level. But for now, the demands of my running take priority in terms of my nutrition.

• **A good running diet has the variety and quality that underlie a good diet for everyone, runner and nonrunner alike.**

A lot of endurance athletes are very particular about what they eat. You'll hear them say, "I've got to have this, I've got to have that" and "I can't eat this, I can't eat that." That's definitely not me.

Don't get me wrong—I take nutrition very seriously. I consider it one of the key factors in running my best. But for me that means eating a well-balanced diet of fresh, high-quality foods instead of processed foods and enjoying my meals while not pigging out just because I run a lot.

I think about diet sort of how I think about training: There are basic elements that will work best for almost everyone. Start with those basics, but don't be afraid to tweak things to find what works best for you. If someone presents something that's pretty far away from the basics as "the key" or "a secret," be skeptical and do your homework. At the same time, don't tell others, "Because this worked for me, it's going to work for you."

One area where maybe I'm different is in regard to carbohydrates. I love bread and, like a lot of runners, used to equate refueling with loading up on carbs. But research has shown that recovery after hard training is helped by adding some high-quality protein to the carbs you're eating. I have a small amount of protein in each of my main meals of the day. Again, it's about balance—I have rice and chicken, or eggs and vegetables, not just all rice or all eggs. Most runners don't run far enough on a regular basis that bonking or hitting the wall on a training run is a common risk. Enjoy your carbohydrates of choice, but don't eat like you're always carbo loading the night before a marathon.

My three main sources of protein are eggs, red meat, and chicken. I eat eggs most often after my main run of the day, and beef or poultry as part of dinner. The split at dinner is roughly beef 40 percent of the time and chicken 60 percent of the time. I usually have beef with dinner if I've done a long run or hard workout that day, because I

FAST FOOD FOR FAST RUNNERS

WHILE IN HIGH school, I worked briefly at a McDonald's, making french fries. But you won't see me there much these days.

Unlike many people who immigrate to the United States, I never found fast food enticing. Part of that is my upbringing. Eating at home as a family is part of our culture. My mother always cooked everything from scratch; I didn't grow up on canned food or anything like that. (Plus, we didn't have the money for my large family to eat out.) My wife and I have tried to raise our daughters with the same appreciation for fresh, home-cooked meals.

The busiest food line at the Olympic Village is McDonald's. I might go there after my race as a treat. But I've seen some runners there 2 days before the Olympic Marathon. I chalk it up to a lack of knowledge. It's fine with me if my competitors act like nutrition isn't important.

Once in a while my girls will have fast food, such as tacos or chicken nuggets. I go along for the family time but almost always eat at home.

want the extra iron to help speed recovery. On the night before a long run or hard workout, I have chicken, because beef can bother my stomach the next morning when I'm running fast.

I like some seafood, especially shrimp, lobster, and wild salmon. (I avoid farmed salmon, which upsets my stomach.) I also occasionally eat tuna and sardines. But mostly for dinner I have chicken or beef.

I eat organic or naturally raised meat whenever possible. I think it's worth the

COFFEE, TEA, AND ME

I DRINK COFFEE mostly on two occasions—as a social thing when visiting with my mother and on the mornings of hard workouts. When I have coffee with my mother, it's after my main run of the day. This is usually late morning or early afternoon; I try not to have coffee after 2:00 p.m. because any later than that and the caffeine will keep me awake at night.

In terms of running, I'll have a cup about 45 minutes to an hour before doing tempo runs, intervals, and long runs. On those days, I notice and appreciate the performance benefit from caffeine that research has shown—lower perceived effort and greater time to exhaustion at a given pace. But I don't drink coffee on the morning of a race, because I want to avoid stomach issues and the need for pit stops. Instead, I have half to three-quarters of a caffeine pill about an hour before the start time. (Not that this practice hasn't caused problems: At the 2012 Olympic Marathon Trials, the pill remained lodged in my throat for the first 21 miles. When I was finally able to swallow it, I took the lead and won the race.)

I love coffee, but I don't drink it every day, because I'm afraid of getting addicted to it. I don't want to become someone who thinks, "I need coffee to get through the day or feel normal running." I like still being able to notice the difference when I drink coffee before hard workouts. I liken it to how I feel faster in the first few days at sea level after I've been training at altitude.

On non-coffee days, I have tea in the morning, about an hour before I start running. This is usually black tea, which has some caffeine but not nearly as much as coffee. If I feel like I need to have something hot later in the day, I'll have some more tea. If it's after 5:00 p.m., I usually have herbal tea or another type that doesn't have caffeine.

extra cost if you can afford it—it tastes so much better and is free of the drugs and hormones often used in factory farming. I consider the higher price an investment in my health and running.

I include a small amount of healthy fat with most meals. Fat in your diet is necessary for many bodily functions. (And yes, it tastes good.) In addition to the fat that naturally comes from the animal products I eat, including dairy, my main sources include nuts and nut butters, avocados, and olive oil.

I eat vegetables with two meals a day and try to eat five servings of fruit a day. As with meat, I try to eat organic or at least pesticide-free produce as much as possible.

My wife and I are very health conscious, and we want to pass those habits along to our daughters. Part of how we do that is by the example we set with nutrition.

A Typical Day's Diet

Now that I've given you an overview of what I consider to be a good running diet, let me take you through a typical day when I'm training for a marathon.

Before I do, I want to make an important point: These are just examples of the types of things I eat and when and what I think serves as a template for a good running diet. I'm not saying this is what I eat every day or that this is exactly how all

RUNNING AND ALCOHOL

I ALMOST NEVER drink alcohol. Maybe once or twice a year in a social setting I'll accept someone's offer of a beer; then I'll drink three or four sips and leave the rest. On the rare occasions when I have wine, I'll drink half a glass at the most. Mostly in those settings, I drink orange juice or water.

Some of that is from my upbringing. My father never got drunk, but he kept liquor in the house. When we first came to the United States, he had us kids taste some. We said, "Oh, this is yucky. Nasty." He said, "Right. That's why you should never have it." So I never really developed an interest in or curiosity about alcohol.

I also think alcohol and athletes don't mix. Maybe I'm old-fashioned in this belief. I know of many world-class runners who enjoy alcohol. But I don't see how alcohol can help you be at your absolute best as a runner, which is my goal.

If you're one of the many runners who enjoy a post-race beer or a glass of wine with dinner, I'm not against that. Almost any food or drink is okay in moderation. But be sure that you're completely rehydrated from the day's running before you have any alcohol; otherwise, you'll slow your recovery.

FOODS THAT CONFLICT WITH RUNNING

MOST RUNNERS HAVE foods that their taste buds love but their stomachs don't. For me, that's mostly spicy foods. Eritrean food, which is similar to Ethiopian cuisine, uses a lot of spices. I also like Indian and Thai food.

But I often have stomach issues and have to make frequent pit stops during my run the day after eating spicy foods. If I eat a spicy dinner the night before a hard tempo run or an interval workout, I'm asking for trouble. For the most part, I eat blander foods when I'm training hard for an upcoming marathon. I look forward to having more spices when I'm recovering after a marathon.

I've also had issues with the Eritrean bread *taita* or *injera* if the grain used to make it, teff, isn't fresh. Taita or injera is a part of every traditional Eritrean meal; it's used in the same way injera is at Ethiopian meals. If I'm unsure of how fresh it is, I'll have rice or whole wheat pita instead so that I can eat what the rest of my family is eating.

Like many runners, I try to avoid high-fiber foods the day before a long or hard run, for the obvious reasons.

These are the things that, over time, I've noticed can interfere with my running. If you don't yet know your "danger" foods, keep track, especially before hard workouts, long runs, and races, to see what patterns emerge. Then stick to eating those foods on easier running days or when you're not in a buildup for a key race.

runners should eat. You need balance and variety in your diet, in the same way that your training should include long and short runs, fast and slow runs. Any one day is meaningful only in relation to all the days that precede and follow it.

Breakfast is where I have the least variety—I almost always eat toast when I get up. I usually put almond butter or peanut butter on it, but sometimes I have honey. It's usually just one piece, a little something

before my main workout of the day. I have toast at least an hour before I start my run.

I understand that a lot of runners have a more rushed schedule in the morning than I do. You might have to wake up and start your morning run almost immediately. In that case, it can be tough to eat before you run. Experiment to see what types of food (probably bland ones) and what amounts you can tolerate soon before a run. You might feel better on an early-morning tempo run, interval session, or standard run of an hour or more if you've taken in a few hundred calories before.

By the time I'm back from my morning run and I sit down to eat my next meal, it's usually noon. (For what I eat and drink immediately after training, see Chapter 9.) If I've done a hard workout or long run, I usually have an omelet or some other egg dish, because I want to be sure I'm getting a good amount of high-quality protein. I put broccoli, red bell peppers, and other vitamin-rich vegetables in my omelets.

On other days, lunch might be a turkey sandwich or something like a kale salad with nuts and some broken-up pieces of Krave Jerky, which is a beef jerky made from naturally raised cattle. (Krave Jerky is one of my sponsors.) Sometimes I have pancakes or French toast, when I feel like having more of a breakfast-type item even though it's midday. As you can see, in most cases I'm having a good mixture of carbohydrates, protein, and healthy fat rather than just a plateful of carbs or a big hunk of protein.

During the afternoon, I snack on fruits if I feel hungry. My daughters and I look forward to family time over fruits at 3:30 or 4:00 p.m., before I do my second workout.

We try to have dinner as a family as often as possible. Now that my daughters are old enough, we all eat the same food for dinner.

Like I said above, dinner usually includes beef or chicken, plus lots of fresh vegetables. We also have rice, pasta, or bread, depending on the meal. When I'm training seriously, whatever my wife, Yordanos, cooks is based on my needs. (See "Foods That Conflict with Running" on page 89.) I'm not as picky when I'm recovering from a marathon, so Yordanos can be more creative in her cooking then.

I've never been a regular dessert eater—which isn't to say I don't love it. As I'll explain later, whether I eat sweets is largely determined by where I am in a training cycle.

While I've always been careful about my diet, these days I pay that much more attention to nutrition. Now if I have a choice, I'd rather go with whole grain or whole wheat bread over white bread, brown rice instead of white rice, and whole wheat pasta rather than white pasta. When I noticed my metabolism starting to slow in my mid-30s, I realized it made sense to get as many nutrients as possible out of everything I ate. Even with as active as I am, it's hard to justify empty calories.

Which leads to . . .

Weight Control and Running

I MEET a lot of runners at race expos who tell me dramatic weight-loss stories. I always congratulate them and tell them, "Now you've got to maintain it. I know how difficult it can be." They're always appreciative, but they do sometimes look at me like, "What do you know about watching your weight?"

What they might not know is that I have the same struggles as anybody else. I can get out of shape and gain weight quickly. As I'll describe below, in the few months before a marathon I'm especially careful about what and how much I eat. I'm like a prizefighter trying to reach the big day at the ideal blend of strength and lightness. As I'll also describe below, I think this is an approach that could work for a lot of runners in the short time before an important race.

I started noticing my metabolism slowing when I was 34 to 35 years old. This was soon after I'd had a pelvic stress fracture that prevented me from making the 2008 Olympic team. Like I said, that injury motivated me to pay more attention to the quality of my food. But I also had to reconsider how much I was eating. I found that, even with running more than 100 miles a week, I was often 4 or 5 pounds heavier than I should be. That might not sound like much, but it was enough to keep me from meeting my running goals.

Another factor in my weight management is something a lot of longtime runners deal with—running doesn't necessarily burn as many calories as it used to. My smartwatch estimates how many calories I expend on a run; after a 10-miler, it will tell me I burned something like 649 calories. That's significantly less than the standard figure of 100 calories per mile. Over time, I've become so efficient at running that, at least when it comes to calories, it can feel like I'm being penalized.

HOW LEAN IS TOO LEAN?

THE LEAST I'VE weighed as a professional runner is 117 pounds. (In comparison, I weighed 122 when I won the 2014 Boston Marathon.) I thought being so light would help me make my third Olympic team, but instead it wound up contributing to the worst injury of my career.

The 2008 Olympic Marathon Trials were held in November 2007 in Central Park, the day before the New York City Marathon. I'd been second in the Olympics, second at New York City, and third at Boston and New York City, but I'd never won a marathon. I was highly motivated to do everything I could to win that race.

I told myself, "The leaner I am, the better I'll run." By that July, I was down to 117. I felt phenomenal and had some great buildup races at shorter distances. But in the last couple of days before the race, my right hip started to feel a little funny. During the race, the pain became excruciating. I finished eighth, well out of contention for the team. After the race I couldn't walk. I later learned I had a pelvic stress fracture and spent most of the next year rehabbing.

The problem was that I was too lean for too long. When I say I weighed 122 before winning Boston, that doesn't mean I was that weight throughout my buildup to the race. I'm usually a little heavier. Despite being vigilant about my diet before a marathon, I try to leave a little cushion; these days, I'd be concerned if I got below 120, and I wouldn't try to stay in the low 120s indefinitely.

If you're highly motivated to lose a little extra weight soon before a key race, that might help you run faster. But don't try to sustain a weight that your body tells you is unnatural. Being a healthy person is much more important than being a faster runner.

Since I've had to be more careful about watching my weight, here's the approach I use: In the 3 to 4 months before a marathon, I gradually get down to my ideal racing weight, which I consider to be in the low 120s. (I'm 5 foot 5½ inches. I was 5 foot 6 when I had an Afro, but that's going back to my high school prom.) I get to this weight by reducing portions of some foods and eliminating others for those few months. Then, after the marathon, I allow my weight to creep back up. For example, after I won the Boston Marathon, my weight went from 122 to about 130 over a period of several weeks. After a marathon, I still eat what most people would consider a very healthy diet, but I don't evaluate every bite that goes in my mouth like I do before a marathon.

This system works well for me because it allows me to safely get to my best racing weight; I aim to lose a pound or two a week until I reach my goal. But it also allows me to return to a weight that's low without being so low I need to live like a monk to maintain it. I don't consider this yo-yo dieting. It's more moving within a range of roughly 10 pounds, as dictated by my racing schedule.

Watching my weight before a marathon can lead to interesting episodes. On a Sunday, I might run 10 miles before going to church. After church is social time, with coffee and doughnuts. I'll look around and see everybody—small, medium, large—having a doughnut. I think, "None of these people ran 10 miles this morning. And I still have an ElliptiGO ride this afternoon. But I'm almost the only one here not eating a doughnut. How sad is that?" When I tell this to my buddy Rich Levy, he'll say, "Well, that's why you won the Boston Marathon."

If you have a goal that's as meaningful to you as winning Boston was to me, I recommend giving this approach a try. Some people can eat anything and everything and be at their best racing weight, and that's fine. Most of us, including me, can't. We have to set aside that idea of "I run so much, I should eat whatever I want" if we want to do everything possible to meet our goals.

For you, that might mean qualifying for Boston, or breaking 4 hours in the marathon or 1:45 for the half marathon, or taking a minute off your 5-K time. As I said in Chapter 1, the right goal can help you think differently. Instead of "I'm making this sacrifice," you'll think, "I'm making this choice." Always keep your long-term goal in mind. So yes, a doughnut after church would be nice. But not as nice as winning the Boston Marathon.

I lose weight gradually, not by making radical changes to my diet, but by cutting back on some foods and being more careful about my portions. For example, I usually drink tea twice a day. I like tea with a lot of sugar or honey in it. But in the few months before a marathon, I drink it plain. I more or less don't eat baked goods and other

---

WEIGHTY MATTERS

THE MOST I'VE ever weighed is 138. A bone specialist told me that's the weight I should be. But if I were consistently that weight I might as well say good-bye to my professional running career, because I wouldn't be as efficient and fast. At that weight, running would feel more like it does when I resume running after taking a break—it hurts, and my thighs are so big they rub together and chafe.

---

sweets during these periods. I eat frequently, but never so much at once that I feel full. Even with something like fruits, I cut back. I might have half a banana at a time instead of a whole banana.

How do you know if you're eating enough to fuel your training but still making consistent, gradual weight loss possible? Imagine you're tending a fireplace. You never let the fire die; you regularly decide whether it needs another log. But you don't throw the whole woodpile in just because it's there. It's the same thing with nutrition. Don't eat so little or so infrequently that you crash. That's when you're most likely to get in trouble by overeating. That's also not a good way to keep a steady blood-sugar level for running and all the other things you do in a day. At the same time, accept that there will be times when you're going to briefly feel a little hungry. Keep the fire lit but not necessarily roaring at all times.

I weigh myself daily when I'm trying to lose weight. There can be day-to-day variation in the readings, depending on when I

WEIGHT MANAGEMENT WHEN YOU'RE INJURED

ONE OF THE many things that makes being injured so bad is that it's easy to gain weight. Some people can be very disciplined when they're not running; the goal of staying lean motivates them to cut back on their calories to match their reduced activity level.

That's usually not me. If I'm injured and know I'm not going to be able to come back in time before an important race, I often throw in the towel. I figure, "What's the point?" and eat too much, and then 2 weeks later I've gained 10 pounds. I ask myself, "Why did I do that?" Then that just makes me feel that much worse. It can be a vicious cycle.

All the more reason to do the strengthening and stretching exercises in Chapters 6 and 7 to lower your injury risk!

weigh myself, if I'm dehydrated, and so on. I keep track of each day's reading and note whether there was something significant, such as having just eaten, that could have affected the reading. The thing to monitor is the overall trend, not slight short-term fluctuations. Again, the idea is to lose weight in a healthy way, not to rush it. It's the same patient approach that works with training—you go from a long run of 13 miles to 14 or 15, not 22. Have the same faith when dieting that you should toward training, knowing how much can be accomplished through the steady accumulation of small bits of progress.

I've developed a few tricks that help me meet my weight-loss goals.

One is that I drink 32 ounces of water just before dinner to fill my stomach. By sitting down at the table without being ravenous, I eat more slowly, and it's easier to judge how much is the proper amount to eat for that meal.

I share food more often when I'm trying to lose weight. For example, I might hand that other half a banana to one of my daughters. That way, I still satisfy the urge to eat something, but with fewer calories. I also remind myself that just because something is put in front of me, it doesn't mean I have to eat the whole thing. Maybe I'll save some for tomorrow, or maybe I'll offer it to the people I'm eating with.

I've had success with the out-of-sight, out-of-mind approach. I tell my wife and daughters, "You can have your cookies and croissants. Just don't let me see them." They help me by hiding foods they know I've said I'm not going to eat for the next little while. I don't want that stuff to be on my diet all the time. And I can't tell my family not to eat certain foods in front of me. Over time, my daughters have really gotten with the program. They'll see me looking at a dessert or treats and say, "Dad, you're in training. You can't have that." (My middle daughter, Fiyori, takes special interest in what I do as a professional athlete.)

Similarly, I let others put away leftovers after meals. It's easy to say, "I'll just have two or three bites," and the next thing you know, you've eaten the plate clean.

DOS AND DON'TS OF DIET

DO consider diet an important part of your training program.

DON'T think that running a lot means you can eat whatever you want.

DO eat a well-balanced diet of mostly fresh foods.

DON'T be fooled by claims of diet "secrets" for runners.

DO include a small amount of high-quality protein with most meals.

DON'T focus on carbohydrates at the expense of other foods.

DO experiment to find what foods cause you stomach issues on a run.

DON'T try to sustain being extra lean for a long time.

DO make extra effort to be at a good running weight before your goal race.

DON'T worry about a little weight gain after your goal race.

Strengthen like Meb

Simple exercises to help you run better and with less injury

REGULAR STRENGTH training is one of the most important things you can do as a runner. The right exercises can help you run more efficiently, lower your risk of injury, improve your running form, slow aging, and make you leaner. Plus, you'll probably look better. That's a big payoff for as little as an hour of work per week.

Don't worry—I'm not expecting you to go to the gym three times a week and do several bench presses of your weight. The strengthening program that has helped me remain a world-class runner all these years consists of simple, do-anywhere exercises that target the muscles used the most when you run. When you combine these exercises with the stretching program I'll lay out in the next chapter, you'll run faster and feel better doing so because your muscles will work in sync as they're meant to.

RUNNER'S 5-MINUTE WHOLE-BODY STRENGTHENING ROUTINE

WHEN YOU'RE SHORT on time and/or space, do these strengthening exercises from the longer lists in this chapter.

- Dip
- Pushup
- Prone Plank
- Supine Plank
- Side Plank
- Stand on Unstable Surface
- Facedown, Lift Opposite Limbs

Why Strength Training Is So Important for Runners

I CAN always tell by looking at race photos when I haven't been as dedicated to strength training as I should be. To take just one example, I'll notice that I'm bent forward at the waist. Among other things, this means I'm using more energy just to keep my back upright. As a result, I'm slower but feel like I'm working harder.

Having better form—and therefore running more efficiently and faster—is one reason strength training is so important. You might ask, "Doesn't running get my legs strong enough?" Yes and no. Yes in that they'll be strong enough to get you through a distance run. But no in that over time, most of us develop imbalances that can impede our efficiency. That can lead to form deteriorating during a run. You see this especially in marathons, where many runners start to break down after 17 or 18 miles because their calves or their quads or something lack the strength to carry them with good form the whole way.

Over time, these weaknesses and imbalances can lead to injury. Your body will start to compensate for a lack of strength in one area by shifting some of the work elsewhere. That usually leads to muscles or tendons getting overloaded as they chronically take on more work than they're designed to handle.

That's especially true if, like many modern runners, you spend a lot of your nonrunning time sitting. Being sedentary for several hours a day both tightens and weakens the large muscles along the back of your body, such as the hamstrings and glutes, that are crucial to running with good form.

Also, notice that in the example above, where I'm bent over at the waist, weakness in my core affects what my legs are doing. The body's movements are interrelated. You don't use just your legs when you run—your arms are swinging back and forth, your core is working to keep your back erect. It all goes hand in hand. You need to have the appropriate strength in those areas as well to run at your best.

Strength training will also help you be leaner. Running will trim you down, but strength training will give you that little extra bit of lean muscularity. That's helpful not just for running but for daily life, especially as we age and start to lose muscle mass (see "Strength Training and Aging" on page 100). And let's be honest—part of the fun of working out is looking good and feeling good about yourself. Strength training is a big help here, even if, as we're about to see, the strength training I think runners should do is different from traditional weight lifting.

The Best Strength Training for Runners

WHEN I was in college, I did what a lot of us who are active have done at some point—I got caught up in how much weight I could lift in the gym. On the bench press, once I could lift more than my body weight, I kept trying to increase the number of reps I could do at that weight.

Eventually I had the insight that this wasn't the best use of my time. I was training to win NCAA championships, not to be a weight lifter. I realized I needed to strengthen my muscles, joints, ligaments, and tendons so I wouldn't get injured. Not only was the heavy lifting at the gym failing to really help with that, but it was also packing on upper-body muscle that I didn't need to run a good 10-K on the track. (When I do heavy lifting, I put on muscle easily. Even today, if you look at me on the start line, I have broader shoulders and a bigger chest than my fellow world-class marathoners.)

After college, I shifted to the type of strength training I still do today. The main exercises I do are shown and described later in this chapter. The goal is to build functional strength—the proper balance of

STRENGTH TRAINING AND AGING

WATCH KIDS PLAY in a park and you'll see them easily moving to the left or right, then running straight, then sideways again, then backward. They naturally have the agility and functional strength to move in any direction.

Most of us lose that as we age. We stop doing activities that require those sorts of movements. Almost everything we do is forward-oriented—walking, running, driving, sitting in front of a computer. To move like our kids do without getting hurt, we have to do extra things that give us the functionality we had more naturally when we were young.

That's been my approach to strength training as I've gotten older. Because I'm not as strong or agile as I was when I was 25, one of my emphases has become countering what aging and daily life do to how I move. For example, sometimes when I go up or down stairs, I walk backward. That works the muscles I otherwise don't use much anymore, whereas when I

was younger they'd get worked if I was goofing around. The same is true of moving laterally. That's why some of the form drills in Chapter 2 involve moving sideways and why some of the exercises in this chapter target muscles along the sides of the body.

I've definitely lost muscle mass, compared with what I had in my 20s. That's natural. You have to work with your body rather than beat yourself up over it. Commit to doing the extra work to counteract what happens with age. For me, that doesn't mean going back to my UCLA days and seeing how much I can bench-press. It means being diligent about strengthening, including doing what seem like weird things, like walking backward. Look at it this way: I'm never going to feel as strong as I did in my late 20s, which is when I won the silver medal at the Olympics. But you know what? Ten years later, I won the Boston Marathon in a personal best. There are always new things you can do to improve.

strength in the key muscles you use while running so you can run with good form, be more efficient, and minimize injury.

The muscles you're targeting with these running-specific exercises aren't necessarily "beach muscles," the ones that people take pride in showing off. (See "About My Six-Pack Abs," opposite.) For example, one of the exercises shown involves pushing a soft, small ball against the wall with your forehead. This strengthens the muscles in the front of your neck so you can hold your head correctly when you run instead of thrusting it forward, which throws off your form. Nobody goes around flexing their

neck muscles, but having the proper strength there is more important for good running than being able to bench-press your body weight five times.

You'll see that some of the exercises I do are balance exercises. They're a great example of working on functional strength. Balance exercises strengthen the small stabilizer muscles in your hips, feet, and elsewhere. When these muscles are working well, your pelvis remains more level when you run, and you have a lot less wasted motion.

I also do a fair amount of work on an exercise ball, also called a Swiss ball. These exercises strengthen my core muscles and

ABOUT MY SIX-PACK ABS

YOU MAY HAVE seen photos of me over the years with six-pack abs. Aren't I contradicting myself by looking like this while saying, "Don't worry about your beach muscles"?

There are times, such as before I won the Boston Marathon, when I'm very lean. The combination of really low body fat, regular core strengthening, and my tendency to build muscle can result in my looking ripped. Like a lot of people, I take some pride in that.

But I also know it's not necessarily the key to good running. From the summer of 2007 up to the Olympic Marathon Trials in November 2007, I was probably the fittest I've ever been. I was superlean during that time and had great definition in my abs. But looks can be deceiving. I was too lean for too long, wound up suffering a pelvic stress fracture during the Trials race, and didn't make the Olympic team. Despite my appearance, my deeper abdominal muscles weren't functioning properly.

Don't be ashamed about looking good, but don't concentrate on that at the expense of functional strength.

There are less obvious ways to learn where you need work. Say you're running and you need to move from the street to the sidewalk. Notice which leg you instinctively lead with. If it's always the same one, that's an indication that the leg you're leading with is stronger. Without your having to think about it, your body is telling you, "I'm more comfortable leading with that leg." You might also discover imbalances like this when you do the exercises and find that one leg tires sooner than the other. Most of us have a dominant leg, just like most of us have a dominant hand. Do a few more reps on your weaker side to try to even things up.

The Best Time to Strength Train

train them to work in sync. That helps your running more than just doing crunches every day and consider that core strengthening, which is what a lot of people do.

You can get clues on what to focus on in your strength training during your runs. If your shoulders are always tired at the end of a long run, or if your hips start bothering you or your hamstrings tighten up, these are indicators you need to pay special attention to those areas.

I USUALLY do my strength training when I'm done with my aerobic workouts for the day. When I was a member of the Mammoth Track Club, we met at the gym 6 afternoons a week for this purpose. I've mostly stayed on that schedule now that I train almost entirely on my own.

But I also like to make good use of pockets of time throughout the day. With strength training, you can get a lot accomplished in a few minutes.

Find what works best for you in terms of scheduling. That might be after your run, it might be a few minutes a few times a day, it might be a separate longer session hours before or after your run. The key is to do the work regularly. If you can do the exercises for at least one body area every day, that will mean hitting them all at least twice a week. That's a good goal for building and maintaining the functional strength you need to run your best.

If you have a chronic problem area, like weak hips and glutes from sitting too much, try to target those areas at least three times a week. Stick with that schedule even when it seems the problem has improved. It's common to be dedicated about strengthening when you're rehabbing from an injury, and then to slack off when it gets better. It's also common for the problem to crop up again a few months after you've stopped working on it. Better to keep addressing it. Remember—prehab, not rehab.

Try not to regularly schedule strength training too soon before a run, especially your harder and longer runs. You don't want to enter those key running sessions overly fatigued.

STRENGTHENING DOS AND DON'TS

DO make strength training an integral part of your training program.

DO focus on functional strength instead of "beach muscles."

DO include upper-body exercises in your program.

DO monitor your body for signs of imbalance or weakness.

DO consider strength training to be that much more important as you age.

DON'T worry about things like how much you can bench-press.

DON'T equate "core strength" only with your abs.

DON'T let strength training detract from your most important running workouts.

DON'T be ashamed about feeling good about how you look.

DON'T be committed to strength training only when you're getting over an injury.

Upper-Body Strengthening Exercises

These first few exercises target your shoulders, chest, and upper back, where having greater strength will help you maintain good posture even as you tire while running.

Pushup

Position yourself on your palms and toes, with your arms straight and your body aligned from your head to your ankles. Slowly lower yourself until your nose is near the ground, then push yourself back up. Try to keep your elbows under your body instead of flared out to the sides. Do 10 to 20 pushups. For a challenging variation, form a triangle with your hands and keep them under your head. For even more of a challenge, form a triangle with your hands and keep them in front of your head.

Incline Pushup

Get in the starting pushup position as described at left, but rest your toes on a raised surface. (How high the surface should be depends on your strength. At first, use a height low enough to ensure that you can maintain good trunk position throughout.) Do 10 to 20 pushups.

Dip

Place your palms behind you on a sturdy surface that's about 2 feet high. Balance yourself on your palms and the backs of your heels, with your legs straight out in front of you. Lower yourself as far as you can, then push back up to the starting position. Do 10 to 20 reps.

The next several exercises strengthen your core, by which I mean all the muscles of your mid-section instead of just your abs. A strong core helps you run with a level pelvis, thereby increasing efficiency and lowering injury risk.

Prone Plank

Balance on your forearms and toes on the floor, with your elbows bent at 90 degrees. Keep a straight line from your shoulders to your ankles, and keep your hips level. Hold for 30 seconds. Over time, work up to holding this position for 1 minute. To make the exercise more challenging, do it with one leg slightly raised off the ground.

Prone Plank Standing on Hands

Get in the Prone Plank position, but straighten your arms and rest some of your weight on your hands. Hold for 30 seconds. Over time, work up to holding the position for 1 minute.

Prone Plank Standing on One Hand and Rotating

Get in the Prone Plank Standing on Hands position. Lift your right hand toward the sky while you turn to the right, so that your upper body rotates close to 90 degrees. Do 10 on each arm.

Prone Plank with High Leg

Get in the basic Prone Plank position. Raise your right leg off the ground and bend it to 90 degrees, and then lift it as high as you can. Do for 30 seconds on each leg.

Supine Plank

Balance on your elbows and heels, with your belly button pointing up. Keep a straight line from your shoulders to your feet. Tuck your chin slightly toward your chest. Hold for 30 seconds. Over time, work up to holding for 1 minute. To make the exercise more challenging, do it with one leg slightly raised off the ground.

Supine Plank Standing on Hands

Get in the Supine Plank position, but straighten your arms, with your fingers pointing toward your body. Hold for 30 seconds. Over time, work up to holding for 1 minute.

Side Plank

Balance yourself on your left elbow and foot, with your right foot resting on your left foot. Place your right hand on your waist. Keep a straight line from your right shoulder to your feet; don't allow your hips to drop. Hold for 30 seconds on each side. Over time, work up to holding for 1 minute. You can make more challenging variations by balancing on your hand instead of your elbow, rotating your upper body, lifting your top leg, and otherwise adding more instability to the basic position.

Crunch, Come Up One Vertebra at a Time

Lie on your back with your knees bent and your feet flat on the floor. Contract your abdominal muscles to slowly raise yourself, coming up one vertebra at a time. Do 10 times.

Crunch, Come Up Crisscross

Lie on your back with your knees bent and feet flat on the floor. Extend your arms with one hand atop the other. Contract your abdominal muscles to slowly raise yourself. While coming up, twist slightly to the right and place your hands by your right hip. Hold for a count of 3 before returning to the start position. Do 10 times on each side.

Crunch, Raise Only Head

Lie on your back with your knees bent and feet flat on the floor. Place your hands behind your head. Use your front neck muscles to raise your head and bring your chin toward your chest. Do 10 times.

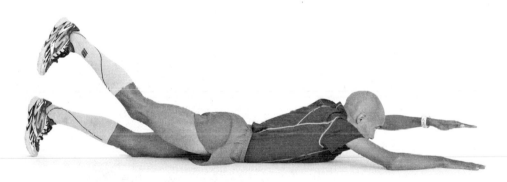

Facedown, Lift Opposite Limbs

Lie on your belly, holding your arms straight out in front of you. Simultaneously lift your right arm and left leg as high as you can, and then lower. Repeat with your left arm and right leg. Do 10 times on each side.

This last upper-body exercise strengthens the muscles in the front of your neck. When they're strong, you can better maintain good head posture while running. When your head is thrust too far forward—which is common in people who spend a lot time working in front of a screen—your whole running form gets thrown off.

Neck Press

Stand tall near a wall with a small, soft ball between your forehead and the wall. (I mean a ball that's soft, not the kind that's used in the sport of softball.) Push with your forehead to press the ball against the wall for a couple of seconds. Do 10 times.

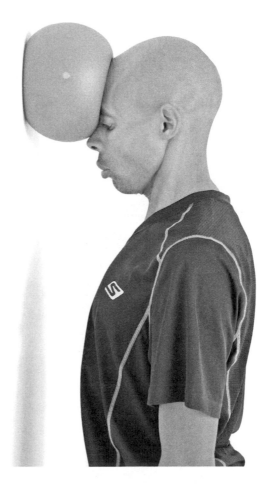

Lower-Body Strengthening Exercises

I do these exercises to strengthen key running muscles, including many of the small stabilizing muscles of the core. Many of them simultaneously improve your balance.

Ankle Weight for Quads

Secure a light ankle weight (5 to 10 pounds) around your right ankle and sit on a Swiss ball. Raise your lower right leg to straighten the leg. Hold at the top of the movement for a couple of seconds while concentrating on contracting the muscles just above your knee. After 10 reps like this, do another 10 with your foot pointed out, then 10 with your foot pointed in. Repeat on the left leg.

Single-Leg Squat, Reach with Opposite Arm for Small Ball

Stand on your right leg, with your knee slightly bent, while holding a small ball in your left hand. While keeping your left foot off the ground, squat to place the ball on the ground in front of you. Pause briefly, then pick up the ball and return to the starting position. Squat again, but place the ball to your left. Do 10 reps while changing the ball's position (center, left, or right) each time. Repeat on your left leg. At first, do the exercise standing on the floor. When that becomes easy, stand on an unstable surface, as shown above.

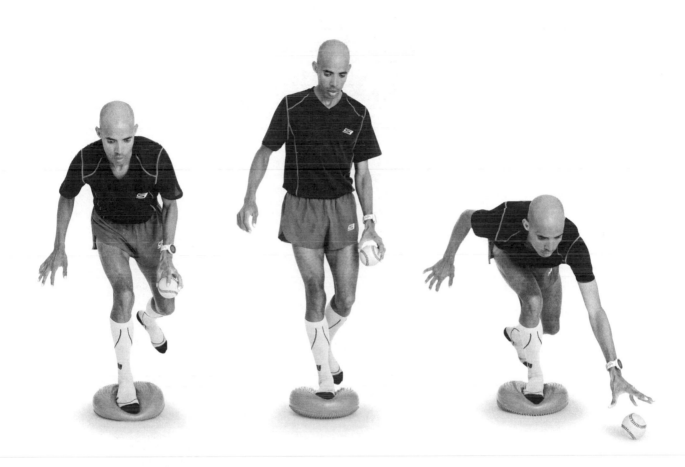

Stand on Unstable Surface

Stand on a DynaDisc, wobble board, pillow, or other unstable surface with your knees slightly bent. Use your glutes and lower abdominal muscles to stabilize yourself. Try to stay standing for 1 minute. When doing so is no longer challenging, stand on one leg at a time.

Squat on Unstable Surface

Stand on a DynaDisc, wobble board, pillow, or other unstable surface with your knees slightly bent. Squat to bring your thighs parallel to the ground. Do 10 squats. When doing so is no longer challenging, squat on one leg at a time.

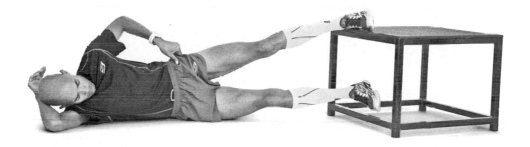

Adductor Strengthen

Lie on your right side with your left foot perched on the edge of a raised surface or the seat of a chair. While keeping your body aligned and your right leg straight, raise your right foot to your left foot, then lower. Do 10 reps on each leg. As you become more familiar with the exercise, do it with a light ankle weight strapped around the lower leg.

Facedown, Straight-Leg Raise as High as Possible

Lie flat on your stomach, with your arms at your sides or your hands under your chin. Using your glutes, lift your right leg as high as possible while keeping it straight; keep your left leg straight and on the ground. Do 10 times with each leg.

Swiss Ball Exercises

Doing exercises on an exercise ball, also called a Swiss ball, results in greater activation of your core muscles. The challenge of stabilizing yourself on the ball also improves your balance.

Sit, Raise Leg

Sit on the ball with your back straight, your hands on your hips, your legs bent at 90 degrees, and your feet flat on the floor. Use the muscles at the top of your right leg to raise your right foot; keep the foot parallel with the floor. Hold for a count of 3 before returning to the start position. Do 10 times on each leg.

Bridge, Lift Legs

Position yourself with your shoulders on the ball, your knees bent at 90 degrees, and your feet flat on the floor. Lift your right foot to extend that leg straight in front of you. Repeat with the left leg. Do 10 times for each leg.

Hamstring Push-Out

Lie faceup with your head and shoulders on the ground and your knees bent so that the bottoms of your feet are flat on the ball. While keeping your feet in place, push the ball away from you to extend your legs. Return to the starting position. Do 10 times. To make this exercise more challenging, push out with one foot at a time while the other leg is raised above the ball and not touching it. Do 10 times with each leg.

Ball Bird Dog

Position yourself on the ball facing downward, with your weight centered on your stomach and your arms dangling toward the ground. Extend your right arm and left leg simultaneously, then do the same with your left arm and right leg. Do 10 reaches with each pair of limbs.

Ball Hamstring Curl

Secure a light ankle weight (5 to 10 pounds) around one of your ankles. Position yourself on the ball facing downward, with your weight centered on your stomach and the balls of your feet on the ground. Bring the weighted leg's foot as close as you can to your butt. Do 10 reps with each leg.

Upward Upper Body

Position yourself on the ball facing downward, with your weight centered on your stomach and the balls of your feet on the ground. Lace your fingers behind your head. Slowly raise your upper body off the ball by arching your lower back. Do 10 times.

Ball Scissors

Position yourself on the ball facing downward, with your weight centered on your stomach and your hands on the floor. Raise your legs straight behind you, and then raise your right leg as high as you can. While lowering your right leg, raise your left leg as high as you can. Alternate leg raises to do 10 times with each leg.

V Spread

Position yourself on the ball facing downward, with your weight centered on your stomach and the balls of your feet on the ground. Raise your legs straight behind you, and then spread them as far apart as you can. Return to the start position. Do 10 times.

Balance on Ball

Put the ball near a table or something else that is waist high and stable. While holding on to the table, position yourself with your knees on top of the ball, but don't latch your feet against the ball. Let go of the table and engage your core muscles to try to balance on top of the ball. If you can work up to 1 minute without grabbing the table, you're a champ!

Crunch from Prone Plank

Get in the starting position for Prone Plank, with your feet wrapped over the top of the Swiss ball and your hands together. While keeping your back straight and your upper body in the starting position, draw the ball toward you by bringing your knees toward the ground. Push the ball back to the starting position. Do 10 times.

Walking

Position yourself on the ball facing downward, with your weight centered on your stomach and your hands and feet on the floor. Moving slowly, reach forward to begin "walking" away from the ball until your feet are on top of it. "Walk" your way back to the starting position in reverse just as slowly. Go up and back 10 times.

These last two exercises use the Swiss ball to increase stretches. The instability of the ball adds a strengthening element.

Bridge

While lying faceup on the ball, center the ball against your lower back. Bring the soles of your feet and the palms of your hands, with your fingers above your head and facing away from you, as close to flat on the ground as possible. Hold for 30 seconds.

Hurdler's Stretch

Sit on the ball with your left leg bent and resting on the ground and your right leg tucked behind you and resting on the ball. Exhale while you lean over and reach for your left foot. Hold for 10 seconds. Repeat with your right leg extended and your left leg tucked.

Stretch like Meb

Why and how to regularly work on your flexibility

I STRETCH daily, usually a few times a day. Being dedicated about stretching helps me run faster and feel better and gave me the longevity to win the Boston Marathon 10 years after I won the silver medal in the 2004 Olympic Marathon.

You can get these same benefits from stretching, even in the likely scenario that you can't devote as much time to it as I do. Later in this chapter you'll see the key stretches I do on a regular basis and when I do them, such as before running, after a hard workout, and so on. But before we get to those descriptions, I want to share my general thoughts on how stretching regularly will help your running.

Why Stretching Is So Important

SINCE HIGH school, I've been fortunate to have coaches who have understood and stressed the importance of regular stretching. My coaches and I can't argue with the people who cite this or that study that says stretching is bad for runners. We can just tell you what has worked, what feels best, and what has contributed to the long careers of many top runners, including me.

When you think about it, stretching before a run is no different from what you

5-MINUTE DO-ANYWHERE LOOSEN-UP ROUTINE

FROM THE LONGER lists of stretches in this chapter, here are some you can do almost anywhere. I like to do a short stretching routine like this when I've been sedentary for a long time, such as during a lengthy plane ride or after a day of meetings. On flights, I go to the back of the plane to stretch if possible, but you can make do in your seat.

Adductor Stretch
Toe-Touch Crossover
Toe-Touch Hamstring Stretch
Toe-Touch Hamstring Stretch after Walking Backward
Reach Oblique
Calf Stretch
Standing Hip Rotation Stretch

STRETCHING AFTER A RUN IS A TIME TO REFLECT ON THE WORK I JUST DID.

see in nature. On television, if you watch nature shows, what do you see? Animals stretch, and then they start moving. Our body's instinct is to gradually switch from inactivity to activity.

Of course you can start a run without stretching first. But I would rather feel better than feel worse starting out. Doing a few minutes of gentle activity to wake up my muscles before I run helps with that.

After a run, stretching also feels natural. Your body is warm, your muscles are loose. Like putting a car in neutral before turning it off, after a run you want to help things settle down and transition to being less active. I love stretching after a run, when I feel energized and have time to reflect on the good work I just did. I feel a sense of great accomplishment. It's a special time of the day for me, almost like a form of meditation.

I firmly believe that post-run stretching lessens the soreness and tightness that can come from running. Over time, that should make you less injury-prone. When you wake up tomorrow, you're going to be feeling a lot better if you stretch after today's run than if you finish your run, rush off to work, and sit all day. I certainly know the feeling of finishing a run, getting busy with something else, maybe driving somewhere, and the next day thinking, "Hmm, why is my hamstring so tight today?" I've tried to learn from those instances as part of my "prehab, not rehab" philosophy.

PRE-RUN STRETCHING MORE IMPORTANT THAN EVER

FOR BIG RACES, I usually stay in a hotel where the event organizers are housing most of the professional runners. In the days before and after the race, it's common to meet other pros in the lobby and go for easy runs together. When I was in my 20s, I had no problem doing these runs impromptu—I'd connect with someone and we'd say, "Meet you in the lobby in 5 or 10 minutes."

I can't do that anymore. As I've gotten older, my pre-run flexibility routine has become so much more important than it used to be. I need that extra time to slowly go through the exercises and get my body ready to run.

That's also why I don't often run with others when I'm home in San Diego. There are some local guys who have asked me to run with them on my recovery days. But say they run at 6:30 in the morning before work; that would mean getting up at 5:30 to do my stretching to be able to meet them. If I slept in a bit and didn't do my stretching, I'd feel it on that run. And if I didn't stretch for a few days, I would constantly feel the difference.

One of the benefits of my profession is that I can usually take my time before a run and head out only when I'm ready. That's probably not your situation, and you might think, "I'm busy—I don't have time for lots of pre-run stretching." But if, like me, you're not as young as you used to be, spending a few minutes a day now will save you lots of time later—time not spent being injured, time not spent feeling sore and creaky all the time. It's when we rush that we older runners often get in trouble.

STRETCHING FOR THE REST OF YOUR LIFE

I ALWAYS TELL people, if you want to know what it's like to be 80, run a marathon. That's usually how I feel for a day or two after I run a marathon—I can't reach for something on the ground, and I have a hard time getting out of a chair.

For me, that's an extreme circumstance. My muscles are shot, but I know it's temporary. But I see a lot of people who aren't in their 80s who live like this all the time. At restaurants or in airports, I see too many people of a wide range of ages who have trouble with the simplest motions. Contrast that with a lot of people I know in their 60s and 70s who stretch regularly and have great range of motion.

Most of us will not continue to be runners until the day we die. But while we're runners, we can get in the habit of regular stretching and keep that up for the rest of our lives. The more we stretch, the more flexible that we are, the more mobile and independent we're going to be. And that's the ultimate goal.

Not all professional runners share my opinion about the importance of regular stretching. I think part of that is because they were successful from a young age and think, "I'm naturally talented." And maybe they never got in the habit of doing much more than running. But you don't see most of them still setting personal bests in their late 30s. I've been asked by some of them, "How do you do it? How did you win Boston just before you turned 39? I'm so achy in the morning these days!" It's because I stick to what works, including regular stretching. If you look at other distance runners who have had long careers, like Olympic medalists Haile Gebrselassie or Bernard Lagat, you'll see that most of them spend time on exercises in addition to their running.

A regular stretching program will help you at least as much as it will help professional runners. After all, we usually don't have to squeeze in our runs before or after sitting at a desk or being on our feet 40 or more hours a week. What we all share is a love of running, of being unhappy when we can't run, and of wanting to know what we can do to minimize time away from running. Stretching is one of those ways, especially as we get older and spend more time sitting.

Try to make stretching like brushing your teeth—a habit or ritual you do daily, without question, that makes you feel better on that day and has cumulative long-term benefits.

When to Stretch

Like I said, I usually stretch a few times a day. Later in this chapter you'll see the flexibility routines I do before a run, after a run, and before a hard workout or race once I've done a warmup jog.

I realize a lot of people can't devote as much time to stretching as I do. But stretching is definitely one of those things where some is better than none. Maybe you can't spend 10 minutes stretching before a run

WHEN NOT TO STRETCH

SOMETIMES, STRETCHING CAN makes things worse, not better. That's often the case when you have an obvious injury. The area that you've injured is already inflamed; stretching the soft tissue around that area can increase the inflammation and prolong your recovery time. I made that mistake when I had a pelvic stress fracture in late 2007 and early 2008. I was so eager to do everything possible to get better. But now I realize that some of the stretching I did delayed rather than shortened my return to running.

This is a good principle to keep in mind even if you don't have an injury as severe as a pelvic stress fracture. My litmus test: If I have an area that feels "off," like hamstring tightness or Achilles tightness, and my instinct is to grab it to feel what's going on there, then I don't stretch it. That instinct to touch the area is a signal from the brain that there's a tension there that's different from normal temporary tightness. Stretching usually makes those sorts of strains worse.

Gently easing into activity and icing after your workout are better choices in those situations. But keep up with the rest of your stretching program even when you're not stretching a troublesome area.

and another 15 minutes after. But I bet you can find 2 or 3 minutes before and 5 minutes after. And some days maybe you'll have more time and can do my full routine.

If you absolutely have to choose between stretching before or after your run, go with after. You can always start your run super slow, maybe even walk a little, and work your way up to your normal pace as your body warms up. For me, when I sweat is when I want to stretch. After the high energy of running, I love taking that time to calm my body down.

Ideally, you'll make time to stretch after every run. Even a few minutes, like while you're toasting a bagel or standing in the shower, can help.

I understand the reality of many runners' lives, where you're getting your run in at 5:30 a.m., then hustling to get the kids ready for school and get yourself to work by 8:00. In that case, stretching later in the day is better than not stretching at all. Maybe when you get home from work, you can find 10 or 15 minutes to stretch, as a way to calm yourself and transition from one part of the day to the next. Or maybe you can find a few minutes before you go to bed once all your responsibilities are done for the day. That will help you feel less stiffness when you get up the next morning and do it all over again.

A lot of these concepts can be used in your daily life. Stretch when you can at work, on a plane, and in other settings where you'll be sedentary for a long time. Just a couple of minutes every hour or 2 can help you feel better on your next run.

Keep with your stretching program when you're traveling or otherwise out of your routine. Believe me, I know how tempting it is after a long travel day to just flop onto your hotel bed. But I've learned over time that stretching for even just 10 minutes will help undo some of the stress and tightness caused by travel and lead to a better night's sleep.

How to Stretch

THERE ARE many ways to stretch. I tend to use different types at different times, as you'll see in the exercise descriptions later in this chapter.

Many of the exercises I do before running are more movements than what you might consider traditional stretching. But they have the same goal of gently increasing blood flow and getting my body ready to work through a greater range of motion. I also do some more normal-looking stretches, such as for my calves, that involve holding a stretch for several seconds.

After a normal recovery run, or after I've done a warmup jog before a hard workout or race, I like to do active isolated stretching, or what a lot of people call rope stretching. The idea here is that you stretch one muscle group, like your hamstrings, by contracting the opposing muscle group (in this example, your quadriceps) to create motion. Doing so helps relax the muscles you're trying to stretch. You take only a few seconds per motion, and use the rope to guide the motion and slightly extend at the top of the motion. I'll describe this in more detail in the explanations for some of the stretches later in this chapter.

I have a different routine for after a hard workout or race. These are mostly exercises to keep the muscles I've just

PRE-RUN STRETCHING HELPS ME RUN WITH BETTER FORM FROM THE START.

worked hard—hamstrings, hips, glutes—from tightening up.

Whatever type of flexibility work I'm doing, I never stretch to the point of pain. I go only to where I feel a slight tension, and then hold onto that feeling for a few seconds or sometimes longer. After doing a stretch a couple of times, I start to notice that I'm going farther each time to reach that same feeling of slight tension. It's the same progressive effort as when I run, where I finish faster than I start.

Be sure you're not holding your breath when you stretch. Breathing deeply will help get oxygen to the muscles you're stretching and allow you to better elongate them.

Sometimes I close my eyes when I stretch. I picture the body part I'm working

YOGA AND RUNNING

WHEN I WAS in college at UCLA, I took a 10-week yoga class. I've also spent time doing Pilates, especially in 2008 and 2009, when I was returning from a pelvic stress fracture.

Both were eye-openers, especially Pilates. Some of those exercises had me shaking. I would think, "Here I am, a world-class marathoner, and this simple movement is making my legs shake." It reinforced my belief that there are always ways to improve and new things to learn.

Rather than go to regular classes, I most often incorporate some yoga and Pilates exercises into my stretching and strengthening programs. I also incorporate some of their breathing and mindfulness concepts. I try to be in the moment when I'm stretching, concentrating on my breathing and monitoring how my body is feeling as I do the exercises.

If you find it difficult to regularly stretch as much as you'd like, committing to a yoga class once or twice a week could be a good way to boost your flexibility. If possible, schedule the class for at least a few hours before or after your run that day.

STRETCHING DOS AND DON'TS

DO make stretching a regular part of your running program.

DO allot time for stretching when planning a day's run.

DO remember that every little bit of stretching helps.

DO prioritize post-run stretching.

DO pay attention to what your body tells you while you stretch.

DON'T stretch to the point of pain.

DON'T stretch an area where you have an acute muscle strain.

DON'T be afraid to experiment with basic stretches to address your unique needs.

DON'T neglect stretching when you're traveling or otherwise out of your routine.

DON'T accept chronic stiffness and restricted range of motion as givens as you age.

on—my hamstring, my Achilles—and visualize it elongating a little bit more each time I stretch it.

Pay attention to what your body is telling you when you stretch. You might find you're more flexible on one side than the other. Or maybe you'll find you're tight in a place that you don't consider one of your "trouble spots." You can learn a lot about the state of your body and what areas you need to work on when you're stretching.

Flexibility Exercises

The three groups of exercises below are organized by when I do them.

PRE-RUN FLEXIBILITY EXERCISES

These are the exercises I do before recovery runs and warmup jogs for races and hard workouts. They're a gentle way to increase blood flow and range of motion so I can run with good form from the first step.

Squat

Stand tall with your feet shoulder-width apart and pointing straight ahead. While keeping your core engaged and your feet flat on the ground, thrust your arms straight out in front of you and squat to bring your quadriceps parallel to the ground. Do 10.

Single-Leg March

From a tall standing position, anchor your left foot firmly on the ground while you raise your right knee and keep your right foot parallel to the ground. Alternate legs to take 10 small steps in this manner with each leg.

Standing Hip Rotation

Stand tall with your feet together and your hands on your hips. Initiating the movement from your pelvis, move in a circular fashion from your belly to your hips. Do 10 times clockwise, then 10 times counterclockwise.

Adductor Stretch

Stand with your hands on your hips and your feet a little more than shoulder-width apart and pointing straight ahead. While keeping your feet pointing straight ahead and your right leg straight, bend your left knee and step to the left, ending with most of your weight on your left foot. Return to the starting position before stepping laterally to the right. Do 10 times on each leg.

Toe-Touch Crossover

Stand with your legs about shoulder-width apart.
Cross your left foot over your right foot. Bend from
your waist to touch your right foot with both hands.
Switch position so that your right foot is crossed
over your left foot, and touch your left foot with
both hands. Continue alternating, touching each
foot 10 times.

Toe-Touch Hamstring Stretch

Stand with both feet together. Take a step forward with your right leg, and point the toes of your
right foot toward your shin. Bend from your waist to reach for your right foot. Repeat with your left
leg. Do 10 times on each leg.

Toe-Touch Hamstring Stretch after Walking Backward

Stand with both feet together. Take a step backward with your left leg and point the toes of your right foot toward your shin. Bend from your waist to reach for your right foot. Repeat with your left leg. Do 10 times on each leg.

Bird Dog

Get on your hands and knees. Engage your core to keep your back flat and straight. Simultaneously reach out with your left arm and extend your right leg straight behind you. Return to the starting position before repeating the movement with your right arm and left leg. Do 10 reaches with each arm.

Bridge

Lie on your back with your feet flat on the ground and your palms on the ground between your shoulders and ears. Press your feet and hands into the ground and squeeze your glutes to raise your hips and upper body into an arch. Hold for 10 seconds. If this is too challenging, lie with your feet flat on the ground and your arms at your sides. Squeeze your glutes to raise your hips and back while keeping your shoulders on the ground.

Calf Stretch

Sit with your legs straight in front of you. Bring your right foot toward you, with your right heel on the ground just below your left knee. Grab the ball of your right foot with both hands and pull your toes toward your chest. Hold the stretch for a few seconds. Do 10 times with each foot.

Achilles Stretch

Start in the same position as for Calf Stretch but with your right heel close to your groin. Grab the ball of your right foot with both hands and pull your toes toward your chest. Hold the stretch for a few seconds. Do 10 times with each foot.

Foam Roll Iliotibial Band

Lying on your side with your bottom leg straight, support yourself with your lower arms so you're perpendicular to a foam roller. Slowly lower your weight onto the roller to the point of moderate pressure (but not pain). Use your arms to shift your position so the outside of your upper leg moves along the roller. Do for 30 seconds on each leg.

PRE–HARD WORKOUT PRERACE/
POST–RECOVERY RUN ROPE STRETCHES

On the day of a race or hard workout, I do these stretches after my warmup jog. On recovery days, I do them after my run.

These exercises are examples of active isolated stretching (AIS), or what some people call rope stretching. The idea behind AIS is that, by contracting one muscle group (for example, your quadriceps), you relax the opposing muscle group (in this example, your hamstrings); doing so allows you to stretch the relaxed muscle group without it going into a protective reflex that can inhibit its elongation.

For all these stretches, the active stretching part lasts only 2 or 3 seconds. Use a rope (or towel or yoga strap) only to guide the motion and extend the stretch at the end of your range of motion. Don't use the rope to pull your legs harshly through the desired range of motion. Exhale forcefully during the short stretch section of each exercise.

Lower Hamstring

Lie on your back with both feet flat on the floor. Raise your right leg to a 90-degree angle, and wrap the rope around the arch of your right foot. While keeping your right thigh perpendicular to the ground, straighten your right leg by contracting your quadriceps. Return your leg to a 90-degree angle. Do 10 on each leg.

Straight-Leg Hamstring

Wrap the rope around the arch of your right foot. Lie on your back with your left foot flat on the ground and your right leg extended straight out in front of you. Contract your right quadriceps to bring that leg as close to perpendicular as you can without strain. Return your leg to the starting position. Do 10 on each leg.

Inner Hamstring

Wrap the rope around your right arch, and then wrap it around your inside right ankle. Lie on your back with your left foot flat on the ground, your right leg extended straight out in front of you, and your right foot turned slightly inward. Keeping your foot turned in, contract your quadriceps to raise your right leg. Return your leg to the starting position. Do 10 on each leg.

Outer Hamstring

Wrap the rope around your right arch, and then wrap it around your outside right ankle. Lie on your back with your left foot flat on the ground, your right leg extended straight out in front of you, and your right foot turned slightly outward. Keeping your foot turned out, contract your quadriceps to raise your right leg. Return your leg to the starting position. Do 10 on each leg.

Adductor

Lie on your back with your legs extended straight out in front of you and your toes pointing slightly toward each other. Wrap the rope around the arch of your right foot, and then wrap it around the inside of your right ankle. Use your inner thigh muscles to swing your right leg out to the side; keep your foot low to the ground and toes pointed slightly inward. Return your leg to the starting position. Do 10 on each leg.

Piriformis Stretch

Lie on your back with your right lower leg crossed over your left knee. Reach under your right leg to grab your left knee with both hands. Pull your left knee toward your chest until you feel a gentle stretch in your right glute. Hold for a count of 3. Do 10 times on each leg.

Quadriceps

Lie on your right side in a fetal position with your knees together and close to your chest. Wrap the rope around the arch of your right foot and hold it with your right hand. If your quads are flexible enough, you can hold your right foot with your right hand instead of using the rope. Grab the top of your left ankle with your left hand. Contract your left hamstrings to extend your upper leg and move your left foot toward your butt. Return to the starting position. Do 10 on each leg.

POST-WORKOUT/POST-RACE STRETCHES

I do these exercises after a race or hard workout to undo some of the hamstring, hip, and glute tightness that can follow fast running.

Lateral Leg Swing

Stand with your hands against a wall or other raised surface (such as a car). Swing your left leg to the left, then swing it across your body to the right. You should be able to go a little farther and higher in both directions with each swing. Do 10 swings with each leg.

Reach-for-Toes Hamstring Stretch

Stand next to a wall, and place your right hand on the wall to balance yourself. Swing your right leg as high as you can while simultaneously swinging your left arm toward the toes of your right foot. Do 10 swings with your right leg. Shift position and do 10 swings with your left leg and right arm.

Reach Oblique

Stand with your feet shoulder-width apart. Reach your left arm above you, with the palm facing up and positioned as if you're holding a small plate. Slide your right hand down your right side. Do 10 times on each side.

On Back, Touch Foot to Opposite Hand

Lie flat on your back with your arms perpendicular to your torso. Swing your right leg across your body and try to touch your left hand with your right foot. Alternate leg swings, doing 10 times on each side.

On Stomach, Touch Foot to Opposite Hand

Lie on your stomach with your arms perpendicular to your torso. Swing your right leg behind and across your body and try to touch your left hand with your right foot. Alternate leg swings, doing 10 times on each side.

Hurdle Stretch Rollover

Start in the classic hurdler stretch position, with your right leg straight out in front of you and your left leg tucked behind you. Gently reach for your right foot to stretch your right hamstring for a couple of seconds. As you come up out of the stretch, roll to your right over your right leg. Both legs will briefly be straight out in front of you. Complete the rollover by extending your left leg straight out in front of you and tucking your right leg behind you, and then go directly into reaching for your left foot to stretch your left hamstring. Roll back over to your left to return to your starting position. Do 10 stretches on each leg.

Standing Hip Rotation

Stand tall with your feet together and your hands on your hips. Initiating the movement from your pelvis, move in a circular fashion from your belly to your hips. Do 10 times clockwise, then 10 times counterclockwise.

On Back, Imaginary Bicycle

Lie flat on your back. Lift your legs while keeping your lower back on the ground. Make a cycling motion with your legs. "Spin" each leg 10 times forward, then do 10 spins with each leg as if you're cycling backward.

On Shoulders, Imaginary Bicycle

Start in the same position as in the previous exercise, but then raise most of your body off the floor so that your weight in resting on your shoulders. Hold your waist in your hands. Make a cycling motion with your legs. "Spin" each leg 10 times forward, then do 10 spins with each leg as if you're cycling backward.

Cross-Train like Meb

Why and how to add other aerobic activities to your running

LIKE MOST world-class marathoners, I usually do two aerobic workouts a day, totaling more than 2 hours between the two. Unlike most world-class marathoners, however, I often do one of my workouts on an ElliptiGO, an elliptical bike.

After I won Boston, some people said I was mentioning riding an ElliptiGO only because they're one of my sponsors. But what I said is true—I consider the cross-training I did on an ElliptiGO 4 or 5 days a week a key part of my training for Boston.

CROSS-TRAINING WHEN TRAVELING

ALTHOUGH I HAVE ridden an ElliptiGO in Central Park, I'm not as dedicated about cross-training when I travel. I mostly stick with running and might do a short, easy second run on a day when, if I were home, I would have cross-trained. Or if I'm doing hard intervals or a tempo run, I'll add to my usual warmup and cooldown, and call it a day.

If I'm coming back from injury and need to cross-train, I'll usually find a pool to water run in. Although I'm not a big fan of water running, I prefer that over indoor exercise machines.

You're more likely to see me in hotel gyms stretching or doing core exercises. I'll bike or use an elliptical machine for 10 or 15 minutes to loosen up, and then do my gym work.

The key here is to know yourself and be realistic. Don't beat yourself up for not getting up at 5:00 a.m. to ride an exercise bike in a hotel gym for an hour. Figure out when your travel schedule will allow you to work out, and then make it happen, doing the activity you most want to do.

I say that because I was nearing my 39th birthday when I was doing my hardest training for Boston, and I've had my share of injuries. If I had tried to train like I did before winning the silver medal in the 2004 Olympic Marathon—130 miles a week, with two runs almost every day of the week—I would have broken down. You can't win a race if you don't make it to the start line!

Regularly riding an ElliptiGO gave me most of the cardiovascular benefits of running, but without the pounding. That left me healthy enough to do my key running workouts while also increasing my fitness.

Riding an ElliptiGO is the best cross-training I've found for runners, but it's not the only kind that can help. Before my first ElliptiGO ride in 2012, I frequently biked or ran in the pool (also known as aqua jogging). I've successfully used cycling and water running to stay fit while injured and counting down to race day.

In this chapter, we'll look at aerobic cross-training for runners in two forms—as something you do as a regular part of your training while you're healthy (and to stay healthy) and as a substitute for running when you're injured. I'll also explain why I think regular cross-training makes sense for the majority of runners, who put in less mileage than I do.

CROSS-TRAINING ON AN ELLIPTIGO IS A KEY PART OF MY PROGRAM.

What Is and Isn't Cross-Training

WHEN I talk about cross-training, I mean an aerobic activity that builds cardiovascular fitness. I don't mean the strengthening and stretching exercises I do daily; I consider them key parts of being a healthy runner. That's why they're covered separately, in Chapters 6 and 7.

I also don't mean outdoor activities I do mostly for fun. After I graduated from college in 1998 and moved to San Diego, my good friend Rich Levy would often invite me to join him on a bike ride or to go sailing or kayaking. I'd do my run and then meet up with him. It was more of a social thing than "Let me see how hard I can ride and get my heart rate up." I just love being outside, and these kinds of activities are more to have fun and refresh my mind. It sure beats sitting on the couch.

These days, if my daughters want to go walk around Mission Bay Park, that's a fun family activity, but I don't consider it cross-training. When I get on my ElliptiGO and ride for an hour with my heart rate in the 130s, that's cross-training!

Why to Cross-Train When You're Healthy

I USED to cross-train only when I was injured. Many times, that was before a big race that I needed to be ready for. For example, 7 weeks before I made the 2004 Olympic team in the marathon, I was hurt, and my training was mostly cycling and aqua jogging. By the day of the Trials race, I had been able to do enough running to get through the marathon and finish second; all the cycling and water running kept me fit while I was waiting to be able to run again.

At the 2008 Olympic Marathon Trials, which were held in November 2007, I suffered my worst injury ever, a pelvic stress fracture. Never mind running—that injury was so severe that walking or simply standing was painful, and some days I had to crawl around my house. When I was healthy enough to start cross-training, I hoped, based on my experience before the 2004 Trials, that cycling would be beneficial. I ran out of time before the 2008 Olympic track trials that June—I think with 2 more weeks of running I could have made the 10,000-meter team. But by then, I was a firm

believer in how aerobic workouts other than running could translate into fitness.

At this time, I was nearing my mid-30s and knew that I wanted to try to make the 2012 Olympic team, when I'd be almost 37. I started experimenting with adding cross-training to my routine when I was healthy. I thought this was a better approach than to keep trying to run a set number of miles per week and have a much higher risk of injury. As my wins at the 2012 Olympic Marathon Trials and 2014 Boston Marathon show, this strategy has worked for me—I can stay healthy enough to regularly do the most important running workouts, and I can stay fit enough to race at a high level without as much pounding.

I think the best candidates for doing cross-training when healthy are runners who find themselves in my situation—you have the dedication to train hard, but you feel that your risk of injury is too high once you get above a certain weekly mileage.

For a lot of people, that's about 35 or 40 miles a week. For someone who's busy with work and family and running that much, I would advise a couple of cross-training sessions a week to get an extra fitness boost. Because you're doing these workouts to supplement rather than replace your running, they don't have to be long—45 minutes to an hour is plenty. You might find it easier to squeeze in a couple of additional workouts of that length than to tack on more miles to your run early in the morning, during your lunch break, or after work.

WHY DON'T MORE ELITES CROSS-TRAIN REGULARLY?

MOST OF MY competitors cross-train only when they're injured, if at all. Even among some of the best runners in the world, there's a running-or-nothing mind-set. The thinking is, "I ran my 2 hours today; now it's time to recover." But there's always room for improvement. For me, the commitment isn't to how many miles I run this week but to everything I can do to be a better runner. You'll see me on the floor stretching or icing or doing other exercises throughout the day. I think of cross-training the same way—it's something else I can do in addition to running that's going to make me fitter and keep me healthier.

A few of the more innovative runners are starting to do things differently. Galen Rupp, who won the silver medal at 10,000 meters in the 2012 Olympics and holds the US record for that distance, does a lot of running on an AlterG treadmill. This is a special treadmill that allows you to run at a lower percentage of your body weight, so you get the aerobic benefits of running without as much pounding. That's worked well for him, but I don't like being on a treadmill. For me, the ElliptiGO achieves the same purpose, but I get to be outside. A lot of elite athletes are adopting this new cross-training tool.

If you have a history of injury, consider buying cross-training equipment an investment in your health. This is an example of my philosophy of "prehab, not rehab." A few hundred dollars or more now could mean a lot of money saved later on doctor's appointments, medical tests, and physical therapy. And it could buy you peace of mind, knowing that you're committing to your long-term running health.

Heavier runners are also good candidates for regular cross-training. Someone who weighs 180 pounds is going to feel the pounding of running more than I will. (I weighed 122 pounds a few days before I won the Boston Marathon.) For these runners, cross-training isn't just a way to get in extra cardiovascular work. It can be a way to really build up endurance, because you can do a 90-minute or 2-hour ElliptiGO or bike ride regularly without the injury risk of running that long every week.

The same applies to runners who have had hip surgery, back or joint problems, or other chronic injuries that limit how much they can run. I've met runners like these who say how much they miss being outside for long workouts. With cross-training, you can go as hard and as long as you like and get some of that endorphin rush you used to get from long runs.

A CROSS-TRAINING SESSION WITH MY FRIEND SURESH CHAURUSHIYA.

The Best Forms of Cross-Training for Runners

YOU'VE PROBABLY figured out by now that I'm partial to the ElliptiGO. They're one of my sponsors, but I wouldn't endorse them if I didn't fully believe in them.

I first tried an ElliptiGO in the summer of 2012. One of the executives of the company, Bryce Whiting, took me out for a 10-mile ride. I wore my heart rate monitor and saw that my heart rate was in the 134-to-138 range. That's what it is on my easy days, my recovery runs. I decided to start riding one regularly.

I've found the ElliptiGO to be the closest you can get to running without the pounding. Your calves, hamstrings, quads, and glutes are all working, whereas on a regular bike it's your quads doing almost all the work. I've never had any soreness or injury from the ElliptiGO, and never felt like it's cut into the quality of my running.

Like I said, I've also had a lot of success with traditional bike riding. I've had periods of having to do a lot of water running, too. Both of these are also excellent choices for runners looking to add cross-training to their programs when they're healthy. Using an indoor elliptical machine and putting an ElliptiGO on a stand indoors are also good choices.

Ultimately, it comes down to what you're most likely to do on a regular basis. I like being outside, so when possible I've done cross-training that allows that. But you might live where it's cold or rainy much of the year, or maybe your schedule means that you have to do a lot of your training in the dark. In that case, an indoor option will be a better choice. But before you buy an ElliptiGO or an expensive bike or piece of home indoor equipment, use something enough to decide if it's a good choice for you.

How to Integrate Cross-Training with Running

IN MY buildup to winning the Boston Marathon, I rode the ElliptiGO 4 or 5 days a week. My main use for it was to replace what traditionally had been my second, shorter, easier run of the day.

For example, before the 2004 Olympics, if I had done a hard workout in the morning, I would do an easy 30- to 40-minute run in the afternoon. Before Boston 2014, I would instead ride my ElliptiGO for 45 to 90 minutes later in the day. To make sure I was getting in my running miles, I'd slightly extend my cooldown after my hard workout. On the ElliptiGO, I would ride at an easy to moderate intensity (although it's hilly where I live, so it's impossible to avoid harder efforts going up hills a few times).

Another scenario is that, on my recovery days, I'll do a 10-mile run in the morning and go for a longer ElliptiGO ride (between 1 and 2 hours) later in the day. Here, too, I'm using the ElliptiGO to replace what 10 years ago would have been an easy 4- or 5-mile afternoon run.

Maybe once a week on a recovery day, if I'm feeling really good, I'll run 10 miles in the morning, ride the ElliptiGO around noon, and then do a second short, easy run.

I think this general approach makes sense for runners who want to incorporate cross-training. Use cross-training to add to the fitness you get from your key running workouts, like long runs, tempo runs, and intervals. If you're training to compete, don't try to replace the important running workouts with cross-training.

Keep your cross-training workouts at an easy to moderate intensity so that you get the aerobic benefits but aren't tired when it's time to run hard or long. Depending on what kind of cross-training you're doing, anywhere from 30 to 90 minutes is a good duration. On an ElliptiGO or indoor bike, you can get a good workout at the shorter end of that range. If you're riding a traditional bike outdoors, you'll need to go more like 60 to 90 minutes to make it worthwhile.

Start with adding two cross-training workouts a week. Stick with that for at least a month to see how it feels and to give your body time to adapt. From there you can decide if your schedule and energy level will allow you to add more.

Why to Cross-Train When You're Injured

I'VE HAD my fair share of injuries. Many times they've happened when I have an important race coming up, and I have to stay as fit as possible. Those situations were my first experiences with cross-training.

My first major injury was Achilles tendinitis in 1996 during my sophomore year at UCLA. I spent 9 weeks running in the pool. Under coach Bob Larsen's guidance, I would simulate my regular running program with hard intervals, tempo runs, and long runs, with my long runs in the pool lasting up to 2 hours.

Once I got back to regular running, after just 4 or 5 weeks of running on land, I ran 13:37 for 5,000 meters, a personal best at the time by more than 15 seconds, and I won the Pacific-10 Conference championship. That was a real eye-opener that "Wow,

STAYING MOTIVATED WHEN INJURED

IT CAN BE hard to stay upbeat and dedicated when you're hurt. Even as someone whose livelihood depends on being in great shape, I sometimes find it hard to stay motivated to do all the cross-training and therapy when I'm injured. When you're running well, you're out there sweating and having good runs and seeing how you're heading in the right direction, whereas if you're hurt and doing something like running in the pool, you can feel like you're putting in all this effort and all you're getting from it is smelling like chlorine.

It's really tough, but you've got to believe that cross-training is going to help you and that you're going to come back in better shape than you would if you did nothing, and maybe even fitter than you currently are. Returning to running after injury is hard enough. Tell yourself every time you cross-train that you're making your return easier because you're staying fit and not gaining weight. There's always a light at the end of the tunnel, whether we struggle physically, emotionally, or mentally. We have to be persistent and have faith that there will be a reward.

The hardest part is getting to the gym and getting in the pool or on the ElliptiGO or the bike. But once you're there, you're like, "Okay, let's get this done." If you can find a friend to cross-train with, that will help you with the hardest part—getting started.

Marathon Trials were just 69 days later. This would have been a tough double under any circumstances, but while running New York, I got a huge blister on the ball of my left foot. I could barely walk, much less run. I cross-trained hard on a bike, wearing a Dr. Scholl's doughnut to protect the wound. When I was able to start running again, the Trials race was less than 7 weeks away. And it's not like I immediately was able to get back to my usual marathon training. I told myself I just needed to be fit enough to place in the top three and make my third Olympic team. But as it turned out, I won in 2:09:08, a new personal best by 5 seconds.

So it's obvious to me that, if you're dedicated, cross-training can help you maintain a high level of fitness when you're injured. Most runners don't have those do-or-die races like I do, where I have to be ready to go on such and such date; they're going to hold the Olympic Marathon Trials no matter what kind of shape I'm in. But still, when you're injured, you always think, "I want to get back to my normal running routine as soon as possible." Cross-training is going to make that possible by keeping you aerobically strong, so that when you can resume running, you're not starting from scratch in terms of your cardiovascular fitness.

this stuff really works! All my time in the pool was worth it."

Fifteen years later, I found myself in a similar situation. I ran what was then a personal best of 2:09:13 at the 2011 New York City Marathon. The 2012 Olympic

The Best Forms of Cross-Training for Injured Runners

AN ELLIPTIGO, elliptical machine, bike (regular or stationary indoor), and water running are the best ways to keep your running fitness when you're injured. As I said previously, I believe the ElliptiGO comes the closest to simulating not just the cardiovascular but also muscular demands of running. Because the motion is close to that of running, you might have less of that "this feels really weird" sensation when you start running again.

But not everyone has easy access to an ElliptiGO, a pool for water running, or whatever is needed for the form of cross-training that might best keep you in shape. And you might be injured for "only" a few weeks and can't justify purchasing an expensive piece of exercise equipment. Even more than with cross-training when you're healthy, what's ultimately the best type when you're injured is the activity you're realistically able to do most days.

Some of that will depend on what's available to you. And some of that depends

RETURNING TO RUNNING FROM INJURY

DON'T RUSH BACK into running after an injury. You might have to start with running or even walking a mile, maybe even half a mile. That's okay—it's more than you've been doing! Stop before you feel pain or like you're compensating in your stride for where you've been injured. If you do too much too soon, you'll probably make the old injury flare up, and you might create a new one.

Start slowly and gradually add to your runs—5 or 10 minutes, or maybe a mile—if you remain problem-free. Eventually you'll get to 2 miles, then 3 miles, and more. It's unbelievable what the body can do.

Stick with cross-training, especially the longer and harder workouts, when you're able to start running again after an injury. That will help you stay fitter, and you'll be more likely to ease back into running. Gradually reduce the length and intensity of cross-training as you get back to your normal running routine.

Mentally, don't be too hard on yourself. Sometimes when I've come back from injury, it's not been a pretty sight. My thighs are rubbing against each other and I feel like a beginner. But at least I'm running. Remind yourself of how you felt when you weren't running and it seemed like there'd never be an end to that. Now you're running again. So be happy, focus on making progress slowly, and remind yourself to take care of your body so you don't get injured and have to go through all that again.

on your mind-set. When I've used an indoor elliptical machine or ridden a stationary bike, it's felt like I've been at it for 2 hours, and then I've looked down and seen that it's been only 15 minutes. For me, something that gets me outside, seeing sights and feeling the breeze in my face, has a lot more appeal, which means I'm more likely to do it daily and for long enough to stay fit.

Of course, variety is the spice of life. If you can regularly do more than one type of cross-training when you're injured, mixing things up might help keep you motivated.

You might need to spend a little time getting used to whatever form of cross-training you choose. The first time I tried water running, I did it without a buoyancy belt, and I couldn't go more than a minute or a minute and a half. By the second day, I was going 20 or 30 minutes and was soon up to 2 hours.

How to Cross-Train When You're Injured

When you're healthy, the best use of cross-training is as a supplement to your running, with two or three workouts a week at a moderate intensity.

That changes when you're hurt. Then you're using cross-training to replace your running, and you should try to replicate a hard running week with whatever form of cross-training you're doing.

For example, when I've had to water run or ride a bike for a long time, I've built my cross-training weeks like a normal training week, with a longest workout; a day of short, hard intervals; a longer sustained hard effort; and the rest as easier days.

So I'll have one day where I go 2 to 2½ hours; that's my "long run." On another day, I'll warm up, then go hard but not all out for 20 to 30 minutes; that's my "tempo run." A couple of days after that, I'll do something like five repeats of 5 minutes really hard, with 2 minutes easy in between; those are my "intervals." I've even tried to simulate really short, fast repeats by going pretty much as hard as possible for 30 seconds to 1 minute to help keep my turnover quick. Doing these different types of workouts will keep your different energy systems in good shape.

There's another benefit to planning your cross-training like this when you're injured—it keeps things more interesting. Having harder and easier days, longer and shorter days can lessen that feeling, all too common when you're hurt, that "every day is the same and I'm going to be injured forever."

A heart rate monitor can help you know if you're hitting the right intensity, especially if you wear one running and know what heart rate you're usually at for each kind of workout. Even on your "easy" cross-training days, a heart rate monitor can be useful. Especially if you're new to a cross-training activity, it can be difficult to hit that comfortable-but-working effort level that comes naturally to most runners.

CROSS-TRAINING DOS AND DON'TS

DO consider adding aerobic cross-training to your training program as a way to build your heart and lungs without the pounding of running.

DO use cross-training to supplement your key running workouts.

DO experiment with different forms of cross-training to find the one you most enjoy and are most likely to do on a regular basis.

DO dedicate yourself to cross-training when injured so you don't lose fitness and gain weight.

DO replicate your hard running workouts with cross-training when you're injured.

DON'T replace your key running workouts with cross-training if you're getting ready for a race.

DON'T buy an expensive piece of exercise equipment unless you've been on it enough to know you'll use it regularly.

DON'T cross-train so hard that it interferes with your key running workouts.

DON'T allow yourself to get too down when an injury means you have to cross-train instead of run.

DON'T stop cross-training just because you're able to resume short, easy runs after an injury.

Recover like Meb

What to do
between runs
to get the most
from your training

ALTHOUGH I'VE saved recovery for the last chapter, that doesn't mean I think recovery is unimportant. In fact, recovery is the glue that holds all the elements of your running program together. Without it, you won't get the full benefits of all the hard work you do in training, racing, stretching, and strengthening; instead, you'll get run-down, sick, chronically sore, maybe even injured. That's especially true if, like me, you're not as young as you used to be.

In this chapter, we'll look not only at why you should build recovery into your training but also at what doing so entails. I'll tell you how surprisingly slowly I run some days, and I'll share some of my tricks for what to do after a run to feel fresher for the next one.

Why Recovery Is the Key to Getting Fitter

A LOT of runners don't realize that it's not while you're running that you get in better shape. While training, you stress your cardiovascular system and fatigue your muscles, tendons, ligaments, and bones. Your body's response to any single training session is "Hey, that crazy runner might do that again. I better get ready!" That adaptation is small improvements that are made to the systems that were stressed during your run.

The adaptations that make you fitter can happen only if you temporarily lessen the stress on your body, which is where recovery comes in. This involves two things: not repeating the stress until your body has had a chance to adapt, and doing things soon after a workout to speed the body's return to its normal state.

This principle of stress–recovery–adaptation is key to training for all sports. You don't see football players trying to improve their bench press every day or sprinters maxing out in every workout. We distance runners need to take recovery even more seriously than those athletes. We don't get time-outs. We don't stop during an intense long run to consult our coach. We go the distance day after day.

Ultimately, the purpose of training is to condition yourself to go as long as you can without pain or struggle. As I described in Chapter 3, the best way to do that is to regularly do a few key types of workouts, including intervals, tempo runs, and long runs. Note the word "regularly" there—the key to success is the day-in, day-out performance, the accumulation of little gains. That doesn't happen if you're running tired all the time. You can build that momentum only if you're ready for those important workouts. Being as dedicated to your recovery as you are to your harder workouts will allow you to perform at your max.

What counts as recovery varies widely among runners, based on factors such as weekly mileage, injury history, age, and what's possible within one's schedule. For some runners, a recovery day means no running. At times in my career, it's meant 10 to 12 miles in the morning and 4 to 7 miles in the afternoon. Most regular runners fall between these two extremes.

What different recovery days for different runners have in common is that they're true to the word "recovery." You should feel less tired, not more, at the end of a recovery day than you did when you woke up. If you run, you probably won't feel great starting out, because you went long or hard the day before. But as you progress through a recovery run, you should start to feel looser and a bit more energized. You should finish feeling a little more eager for your next hard or long run.

If you don't run the day after long or hard workouts, consider one of the cross-training options I discussed in Chapter 8. Or maybe set aside a chunk of time for a good stretching session or yoga class. These activities will serve some of the purpose of recovery runs, especially increasing blood flow to help reduce stiffness and soreness. That will usually help you recover faster than doing nothing.

How to Gauge Recovery

OVER TIME, you can learn to read your body's signals to determine how your recovery after a hard day is going. I pay attention to my resting heart rate. If it remains elevated throughout the day, it can be a sign that I'm not recovering like I should be. One rule of thumb is to consider taking extra recovery time if your heart rate is 10 percent higher than it usually is.

Mostly, however, I monitor other signals from my body. (After all, heart rate can be elevated for other reasons, such as if you have had too much caffeine or a night of poor sleep.) Some signals are the obvious, palpable ones. As I go about my business the day after a hard run, I pay attention to how I feel. Is my calf tight? Is my hamstring sore?

There's good pain and there's bad pain. The good kind is that little bit of burning or fatigue that's natural after you've worked hard. Bad pain is more acute, something that makes you think, "That's not right" or makes you move differently. If I feel bad pain in the afternoon after a hard workout, I'll usually heed what my body is telling me and not do a short afternoon run.

You should also monitor your energy level. Throughout the day, notice whether you feel strong or run-down. Of course, an hour after a hard workout, you might be thinking, "No way can I run tomorrow, no matter how easy." But see how you feel once you've rehydrated and refueled and done some of the other recovery practices I'll describe later. If several hours later you feel run-down, like that drained feeling you can have after getting out of a whirlpool bath, you need more recovery. But if over the course of the day you become increasingly upbeat and you feel good walking around doing things, then you'll know you've recovered.

The Art of Recovery Runs

ONE OF the biggest differences between the training of world-class runners and that of recreational runners is how slowly we elites sometimes run. Let me explain.

Let's say it's the day after a hard workout. A typical recovery run for me is 10 miles in 65 minutes. A 10-miler at an average of 6:30 per mile might sound fast, but consider it in perspective. That's almost 2 minutes per mile slower than I can run for a half-marathon and more than 90 seconds per mile slower than my marathon race pace. For someone who runs a 3:30 marathon, which is about 8 minutes per mile, that would be like averaging a 9:30 pace on a recovery day.

Many recreational runners don't have this great a range in the paces they regularly run. You might have some pace per mile you think is too slow, no matter how tired you are. This approach can hold you back in two related ways. First, you might have chronic low-level fatigue because you never really give your body a chance to recover from your hard workouts. Second, when it comes time to run hard, you can't run as fast as you would if you were truly recovered. As a result, you don't get as much benefit as you should from your hard workouts, and your fitness doesn't improve as much.

Be okay with going at a relaxed, untaxing pace on your recovery runs, especially at the beginning. I might start a recovery run at 7:15 per mile. If I'm training at altitude and I did a really long run the day before, it might be more like 7:30 starting out. On that day, that's the pace my body is telling me it's comfortable at as I get going. Usually, as I warm up, the pace will come down over the course of the run. But that's happening because I'm letting the pace come to me, rather than thinking, "By the 3rd mile I need to be running 6:30s, and by the 8th mile I better be at 6:10s, or this run is a waste."

If I feel bad on a recovery run even after the first few miles, I cover the distance I'd planned to, but at a slower pace rather than cutting the run short. Again, I don't have preset notions of what's "too slow." Long term, I'd rather have several runs of 10 or 12 miles at a little slower than usual than have 6- or 8-milers I pressed the pace on when I should have been relaxing. This approach could be helpful especially if you're trying to get past a certain weekly mileage but seem to be stuck. It could be that erring on the side of going a little slower on your recovery days will mean feeling good enough to run longer on them.

If I find I feel great on a recovery day, I hold back instead of pushing the pace. Training is a cumulative process, with all the workouts building on one another up to the key race. Sure, it can be tempting to let it rip when I feel great the day after a long run or interval workout. But I remind myself of my long-term goal. Although it's difficult to do when I feel so fluid, I put on the brakes. I know that what really matters is the next hard workout and that pushing the pace on a recovery day will probably come back to haunt me.

I like to check my mile splits on recovery runs. This might sound contradictory to what I just said about not having preconceived notions of how fast or slow I should be going on recovery days, but it's not.

First, it's just a little game I play with myself. I like to try to guess what my next mile split will be based on how I feel. I'm usually within 10 seconds. It's a fun way to learn how to read your body.

Second, it's good internal information for how recovered I am. I might think, "This next mile will be 6:17," but it turns out to be 6:08. This tells me I've recovered well from the previous day's hard effort. That's not

---

WHERE TO DO RECOVERY RUNS

I AM ALL about routine. That includes where I do my recovery runs.

I could save time by running from my house on my recovery days. But whenever possible, I take a short drive so that I can run on grass. (I live less than 2½ miles from Balboa Park and Mission Bay Park.) I strongly believe that doing recovery runs on soft surfaces has contributed to my having such a long career. The goal is to take it easy and get my body ready for the next long or hard run. Lessening the pounding by avoiding asphalt helps with that.

I think this is especially valuable for older runners. You might not have the time to drive to a place with lots of trails, but most runners can find somewhere nearby with an acceptable soft surface. I'm okay with running multiple loops of a park perimeter so that I can do my whole recovery run on grass. I usually switch direction every few loops to balance things out and get a slightly different view of the scenery.

---

because I'm running at a 6:08 pace but because to my body, that pace felt slower. On the other hand, sometimes after a really long run I'll think, "This next mile will be 6:32," but it turns out to be 6:45. That tells me I'm still very tired and that I should keep the entire run relaxed and make sure I do good recovery practices the rest of the day.

Some runners leave their watches at home on recovery days so they won't be tempted to check their splits and get caught up in running faster than they should. Because I don't have that problem, I think that checking my splits on recovery days boosts my confidence when I'm building up to a key race. I find that I have more days where I think, "This will be a 6:40 mile," and it turns out to be 6:25. When that starts happening more often, I know my fitness is coming along. It's another thing that gives me hope that it's all going to come together on race day.

How to Speed Recovery between Runs

Running is my profession. That means that, although I might run "only" 2 out of 24 hours in a day, most of the things I do when I'm not running ultimately contribute to how well I race. Those things include not just stretching, strengthening, eating a healthy diet, and cross-training but also things I do to speed recovery, especially after a long or hard workout.

Below are some of the key post-run recovery practices I regularly do. If you incorporate some of them into your training program, you'll get more out of the hard work you do running.

POST-WORKOUT NUTRITION. Research has shown that when you do a hard or long workout, your muscles are most receptive to calories in the first 30 to 90 minutes that follow. During this "recovery window," your body soaks up the calories like a sponge and converts them to glycogen, the stored fuel source in your muscles, at up to three times

the normal rate. That leads to your muscles recovering more quickly, and you avoid that dragging feeling that can happen later in the day if you wait too long to refuel.

I've been dedicated to refueling immediately after my longest and hardest workouts for most of my professional career. It became part of my routine early in my time with Running USA California (which became the Mammoth Track Club), when I really started training harder and running more than I had in college. It's not like I suddenly became superhuman from having a sports drink and a banana, PowerBar, or Krave Jerky soon after my workouts. The effect was more subtle, like I could better handle the training because I didn't feel sore or run-down as often.

Bear in mind that I usually have an electrolyte drink during my interval workouts, tempo runs, and long runs. A typical scenario after the hard sessions is that I'll finish whatever's in that bottle, go for my cooldown jog, and then immediately mix 10 ounces of water with a packet of protein-enhanced chocolate-flavored Generation UCAN, a sports drink made by one of my sponsors. I down that immediately, before I start stretching or even chitchatting with others.

After I stretch, I'll have a banana or PowerBar. This means that within 30 minutes of finishing my cooldown, I've already taken in a few hundred calories of a mixture of carbohydrates and protein. Then I go home, where sometimes I'll have warm milk (more carbs and protein), and within maybe

SHORT-TERM MARATHON RECOVERY

RIGHT AFTER A marathon, I don't feel like eating for a while, or at least eating anything substantial. Even with the importance I place on taking in protein soon after a long or hard run, after a marathon I could have a steak placed in front of me and think, "I don't want it right now. That's not appealing."

My body tells me sugar is what it needs right after. If I don't have something really, really sweet, look out—flashing lights and dizziness. After I won Boston, I had some Generation UCAN, because I always pack it with me, and then I had a PowerBar. Things were so hectic the rest of the day that I didn't have a real meal until 9:00 that night. My brother Hawi had some Krave Jerky with him, so we snacked on that, and I drank a lot of tea with honey to keep from crashing.

You'll probably be able to have a real meal sooner than I did. But I recommend doing like I do and packing a few sweet items with your post-race gear. You don't want to find yourself with nothing to eat once your appetite returns.

If the marathon is on a Sunday, I usually don't try to run again until the following Thursday. In the 3 days between, I'll go for walks if I came out of the race with just the normal aches and pains. I know my fellow Boston Marathon champion Bill Rodgers would sometimes run 8 to 12 miles the day after a marathon, which I find amazing. I usually can't even think about running the next day. I often have trouble just walking and sitting, and I walk down stairs backward.

You're the best judge of when to start running again. Let your body, not your mind or your devotion to your training log, be your guide. If you can't even walk normally, then a short, hobbling run isn't going to be in your best interest.

It's better to start up again 1 day later than 1 day early. I felt better after the 2014 New York City Marathon than after any other marathon. I even felt like going for a run the following day. But I held off until the Wednesday after the race (held on a Sunday) just to be safe.

On your first few runs back, don't be committed to going a certain distance no matter how you feel. You might feel okay for 10 or 15 minutes, but then get really tired and start running with bad form. That's going to delay your recovery.

I do some gentle stretching the day after a marathon. Doing so can make me sore, but I tell myself the main goal now is to recover and get ready for the next one. By the 2nd or 3rd day after, a little light stretching helps to increase blood flow to the muscles. A massage in the first few days after a marathon can also expedite recovery and allow you to start moving more smoothly.

After a marathon, I'm ready mentally and physically for a break. I know that's not necessarily the case with other runners. Some people like the challenge of running two marathons in a weekend or a marathon every week for a month. If that's what you want to do, that's fine. But I think if you want longevity in the sport, it's good to give your body a break.

2 hours of finishing my workout, I'll have an omelet or some other meal containing high-quality protein to help with muscle resynthesis.

I keep hydrating throughout the day. I always have a water bottle with me. My goal is to drink a total of about 2 liters of water before dinner. Obviously, how much water you need depends on how much you sweat. I always try to make sure I'm drinking enough water later in the day that my urine is beige or a little bit gold.

ICE AND EPSOM SALTS BATHS. For much of my professional career, ice baths have been my go-to recovery technique after every morning run. When I was a member of the Mammoth Track Club, I achieved the same purpose by standing in a cold mountain stream up to my waist. Sitting or standing in very cold water soon after running reduces inflammation, and that helps speed recovery.

That said, now that I live full-time in San Diego, I don't take ice baths as often as I used to. For a while there, I was going to the store and getting 50 pounds of ice three times a week. I'd take a 15-minute ice bath and then be shivering for the next 3 or 4 hours. Once I even hurt myself carrying all those heavy bags of ice! I thought, "This is ridiculous."

It's not that I no longer believe in the effectiveness of ice baths. But I feel like I'm so dedicated to all the other aspects of recovery that I don't absolutely need to take regular ice baths. However, if you're not able to devote the time to recovery that I am, experiment with 15-minute ice baths after your hardest and longest runs. I think you'll notice the difference the next day. Just be sure to wear a hat while you're in the bath.

In the past year or so, I've started sometimes taking Epsom salts baths instead of ice baths. They sure are a lot more fun. I don't think Epsom salts baths reduce inflammation the way ice baths can, but they're effective at relieving soreness. I use them mostly when I know a hard workout or race is going to make me sore the next day. I feel like the Epsom salts baths make that soreness less drastic.

MASSAGE. Massage has been one of my main forms of recovery for years. I spend a lot of time on massage and related forms of therapy, such as chiropractic care and Active Release Techniques. This form of recovery is so important to me that on gift-giving occasions, some friends and supporters have given me money to devote to therapy.

I usually ask the therapist to work as deep as possible, which can cause me to wonder, "Wait, why am I paying to be in so much pain?"

I do so because I really believe the therapy helps my muscles recover faster. I might be hurting during the session, but I definitely feel better after. I consider regular massage a form of long-term care, one that has helped me have such a lengthy career at the top of the sport.

I most often get massages after hard workouts (intervals or tempo runs) and long runs. When I'm at peak marathon training, I'll get a massage at least twice a week and sometimes three times a week.

I often take advantage of the massages offered after a race. Even though I'm not always familiar with the person who's working on me, I'm okay with this. I ask them not to go too deep, like they might during a normal session; my muscles are already overworked, so I want help oxygenating the tissue more than anything else. If my glutes and hip flexors aren't too "jumpy," I'll ask the therapist to go a little deeper there. The result I'm looking for is the way I feel after a good stretching session, so I won't be as stiff the following day.

Before a race, I'm very particular. I usually don't let anybody touch me the day before. Two days before, I'll sometimes have someone work only on my upper body, doing just a little light work to help me loosen up.

COMPRESSION GEAR. Here's a fun fact: I'm the first man to win the Boston Marathon wearing compression socks.

I've worn compression socks for training and racing since 2003. But I also have them on for most of the rest of the day. (Yes, a different pair than the ones I ran in!) Research has shown that people who wear compression gear after workouts report less exercise-induced muscle soreness. In theory, that should result in being ready to run hard again sooner. It definitely means being more eager for your next workout, because you're not feeling aches and pains as much. I really believe compression gear has helped me in this way. (I wear CEP Compression gear; they're one of my sponsors.)

I also sometimes wear compression boots made by the company NormaTec. These are leg length; once you inflate them, you look like you're ready for a space walk. I most often wear these for about an hour before I go to bed if I've run a hard workout that morning. My muscles are a lot happier and warmer since I've replaced ice baths with compression boots.

POST-RACE RECOVERY

AFTER A RACE of a half-marathon or shorter, my routine isn't that much different from what I do after a hard workout. That includes a cooldown jog and the post-workout/post-race exercises I described in Chapter 7. Ice baths can be difficult to pull off soon after a race, but I do try to ice whatever body parts might be particularly sore.

If it's a shorter race, like a 10-K, I might do a short, easy afternoon run. After a half-marathon, that temptation isn't there. If possible, I try to get some walking in during the afternoon to reduce stiffness.

Eating after a race can be tricky. You might not have an appetite for a while. And, unlike after a hard workout at home, you might not have access to the food you want once you do feel like eating. I always pack a sports drink and snacks, such as a PowerBar, Krave Jerky, and a banana. When I get back to the hotel or wherever I'm staying, I have a high-protein meal like I do after a hard workout, such as an omelet, even though by then it might be 1:00 or 2:00 in the afternoon.

NAPPING AND SLEEPING. Many elite runners nap daily, usually in the early to mid afternoon before their second, easier run of the day. Even a short nap can refresh you and release certain hormones that can help speed recovery.

For the first part of my professional career, I wasn't a napper. It just didn't agree with me when I was younger—on the rare occasions when I took a nap back then, I would wind up not falling asleep that night until midnight or later. And then I'd have to get up at 7:00 the next morning to meet my teammates for training.

That started changing around 2009. Now, with three young girls and such a busy schedule, if I put my head on a pillow, I'm most likely going to go to sleep. Usually it's only for 10 or 15 minutes, but I have napped for as long as 90 minutes. I nap in the midafternoon, starting anywhere from 2:00 p.m. to 3:30 p.m., depending on my schedule.

I took naps more often in the 4 weeks before I won the Boston Marathon. I was altitude training in Mammoth Lakes. My daughters were home in San Diego. I bet you can figure out the connection.

I understand that most runners' schedules don't allow for regular naps. But maybe on the weekends, especially after a long run, you could find time for a short afternoon nap. That should help you feel fresher the next day.

What's more important are good sleep habits. For most of us, our bodies and minds are so active all day. Find things that calm you before bedtime so you can fall asleep easily instead of lying there with your mind racing. I really like to read books at night to help with this.

Sometimes I drink warm milk about an hour before I go to sleep. When I was growing up, warm milk with honey at night was a treat. It definitely helps me fall asleep. I find it especially helpful before a marathon, when I have all this energy because of cutting back my training and my mind is working overtime thinking about the race.

I've never been a guy who sleeps until 10:00 or 11:00 in the morning. I'm a morning person. Even without setting an alarm, I'm usually up by 6:30. (I like to joke that my three young daughters are my alarm clock.) I might sleep a little more if my schedule allowed it, but I wouldn't be one of these 11-hours-a-night sleepers. I can function at a really high level if I regularly get my 7 or 8 hours of sleep a night.

TOOLS AND GADGETS. There are so many products on the market to help runners recover. I've tried some version of almost all of them.

I use many items for self-massage: a foam roller, a PVC pipe, a massage stick, a small ball, a massage roller co-created by elite marathoner Adriana Nelson called ROLL Recovery, and others. I tend to use different ones on different body parts. For example, I work on my iliotibial band and other areas around the knee with the foam roller or PVC pipe (which is harder than the foam roller). For my high glutes, I'll roll a ball around the area while standing next to a wall. It's good to experiment with different products and find which ones provide the most relief to your particular trouble areas.

At the high-tech (and much more expensive) end of things, I've had good results from two devices.

The first is an electrostimulation machine made by Compex. I get stares when I pull it out to use in airports, because it has wires that send positive and negative electrical charges to muscles. This isn't as scary as it might sound—that's what your brain does to tell your muscles to fire. In

this case, you use the machine on body parts like you might a self-massage tool. The idea is that it increases blood flow to the muscles you're targeting, which helps remove waste products and reduce soreness. I've had one since 2010, and it's so well used that it has almost given up on me.

I also have a machine called Human Tecar. It's similar to an ultrasound machine. It stimulates the circulatory system in the area it's being used on, which helps accelerate the body's natural self-repair process. I first used it in 2005, when I ruptured my quad at the world championships. I've been using it regularly since 2010.

Finally, there's my smartwatch. It has a function that uses several factors, including fitness level, age, heart rate, and weight, to estimate how much recovery time you need after a workout. After I do a long run, it might read "23 hours." If, for fun, I wear it on a short jog with one of my daughters, it will read "0 hours."

The idea here isn't that you should base your schedule on what your watch says. But it can be a helpful estimate of when you'll be ready to work out again. As always, you should pay attention to what your body is telling you—do you feel good and ready to push it, or are you dragging and needing to take it easy? Over time, you can track how often the watch's estimate coincides with how you feel. I find it to be a helpful reminder that I'm mortal and that if I want to continue to enjoy my running for years to come, I need to listen to and respect what my body is telling me.

RECOVERY DOS AND DON'TS

DO consider recovery as important as hard workouts and long runs.

DO listen to your body about how far and hard to run.

DO run on soft surfaces on recovery days.

DO take measures throughout the day to speed recovery.

DO bring food with you to races.

DON'T push the pace on recovery days.

DON'T accept always being sore and tired as part of being a runner.

DON'T be afraid to take more recovery days if your body says it needs them.

DON'T go too long without eating after hard workouts.

DON'T rush back into training after a marathon.

ACKNOWLEDGMENTS

From Meb Keflezighi

I would like to acknowledge the many people who have touched my life through sports.

My father, Russom, made time to take us to the park to play soccer and exercise. He told us, "Sports is good for the mind," and he led by example. He was ahead of his time.

Several coaches passed on their passion for running to me:

Coach Dick Lord saw my Olympic potential when I was in 7th grade.

Coach Ed Ramos believed in me from the start, telling me, "Son, you can do this."

Coach Ron Tabb saw my future doing something special at the Olympics. He predicted I would win medals in 2004 and 2008. Ron, you were right on—my New York City and Boston Marathon victories made up for not making the 2008 Olympics.

Coach Manny Bautista gave me a training log and summer running camps.

Paul Greer was the first one to hire me as a coach, in 2000. I had fun working with you but decided to pursue the unfinished business of athletics. I needed to be an athlete at that stage of my running career, and it looks like my coaching career will be put on hold for just a little while longer. . . .

Terrence Mahon challenged me to take my competitiveness to the international level.

Thanks for helping me out with the gym work and physical therapy.

Dan Pfaff realized that as distance runners, we never do anything to increase agility. You taught me it is okay to be a kid again and jump around and move side to side.

Coach Eric Peterson helped me realize that I could still get the best from myself at UCLA.

My main coach of 20 years, Bob Larsen was patient and more concerned with my long-term development than with just winning NCAA titles. Thanks to that vision, we have both accomplished more than we imagined.

And, of course, the legendary coach Joe Vigil, who always said it is not just about running but also about using the 9 inches above the shoulder—the brain.

I learned from all of you to become the versatile runner I am today.

All my teammates in high school, college, and post-collegiate training for all the miles we ran together, and all my competitors and rivals for pushing me to get the best out of myself.

Rich Levy, though I never claimed you as my coach, you have always been there for me. You always lent your time and energy by pacing me on my San Diego workouts and introduced me to kayaking and wind sailing to get my core workout. Since high school and to this day, you encourage me to have fun with the sport.

So many physical therapists have allowed me to use their facilities to strengthen myself. I may have climbed the biggest mountain or conquered the 26.2-mile journey, but I didn't do it alone. Thanks to everyone who helped get me to the start line. It may be small to you, but it was huge to me: Mammoth Sport Center; Dr. Devin Young at Intouch Chiropractic; Gino Cinco at Function Smart Physical Therapy; La Jolla Physical Therapy, with Joel and Suzanne; both Olympic Training Centers, in Colorado Springs, Colorado, and Chula Vista, California; Mario Scerri at Human Tecar for diagnosing my injury in 2005 and supporting me ever since; Dr. Rosen, Dr. Duke, and Jimmy Lynch, my go-to team in New York City for medical, chiropractic, and massage services; Dr. Steve Van Camp, who helped me design my first workouts in high school and taught me about great sportsmen in history, and Gail Van Camp, who helped me learn more about running by writing about it; Dr. Lewis Maharam, who allowed what I call my second career by diagnosing my pelvic stress fracture in 2007.

Also to my bike pacers: Rich Levy, Mario Arce, Dirk Addis, Tomas Rodrigues, Bejan Mahi, Sara Chavez, and Coach Larsen. You made it easy for me, but you also saw me suffer all those miles. I survived the workouts and imagine you in front of me whenever someone in a race makes a move.

To Dr. Krista Austin, who helped me early on with my nutrition and believed I could win titles.

To Mike Anderson, who believed I would be a wonderful marathoner before I knew the distance.

To my siblings for their support. Aklilu and Fitsum, thanks for allowing me to follow in your footsteps. If you guys didn't do sports in high school, I am not sure what I would be doing today.

To Hawi: Brother first and manager second, you always have my best interests at heart. Thanks for making me look good and balanced.

And of course to be an athlete, you have to eat right. Mom knows best, and I am grateful to my mother, Awetash, who fed me and all her kids day in and day out with good nutrition and unconditional love.

To my wife, Yordanos, and our three angels. Thanks for being understanding when I'm not with you, but with my running community, who ask about you guys and appreciate your sharing your husband and father with his supporters all around the world. Yordanos, thanks for all that you do to allow me to do what I love.

Finally, *Runner's World* published an article, "Meb for Mortals," long before the idea for this book arose. Thanks to Rodale for making it possible and to Scott Douglas for all your work to execute the opportunity.

From Scott Douglas

David Willey and Mark Weinstein were early and strong advocates for this book, and David came up with the title.

Stacey Cramp and Chris Kraft were patient and supportive while I worked on this book around my normal *Runner's World* responsibilities.

ABOUT THE AUTHORS

MEB KEFLEZIGHI (pronounced Kef-lez-ghee) secured a place in history and the hearts of millions when he won the emotional 2014 Boston Marathon. Meb's journey from humble beginnings in Eritrea to becoming America's favorite runner has been called one of the best illustrations of the American dream.

Meb has a habit of making history. In 2004, he became the first American man to win an Olympic medal in the marathon since Frank Shorter in 1976. In 2009, Meb became the first American to win the New York City Marathon since Alberto Salazar in 1982. And when Meb won the 2014 Boston Marathon, he became the first American male winner since Greg Meyer in 1983. Meb is the only athlete in history to win the New York City and Boston Marathons and an Olympic Marathon medal.

Beyond his athletic achievements, which include more than 20 national championships and three US Olympic teams, Meb is a motivational speaker, an author, and the founder of the MEB Foundation, which promotes youth health, education, and fitness.

SCOTT DOUGLAS is senior content editor for *Runner's World* and the author or coauthor of six other running books. Scott has run more than 100,000 miles since taking up the sport in 1979. He lives in South Portland, Maine.

ALSO BY MEB KEFLEZIGHI

Run to Overcome (with Dick Patrick)

ALSO BY SCOTT DOUGLAS

Advanced Marathoning (with Pete Pfitzinger)

Bill Rodgers' Lifetime Running Plan (with Bill Rodgers)

The Complete Idiot's Guide to Running (with Bill Rodgers)

The Little Red Book of Running

Road Racing for Serious Runners (with Pete Pfitzinger)

The Runner's World *Complete Guide to Minimalism and Barefoot Running*

INDEX

Boldface page references indicate photographs. <u>Underscored</u> references indicate boxed text.

A

Abdirahman, Abdi, 79–80
Achilles tendinitis, 171
Active isolated stretching (AIS), 70, 149. *See also* Rope stretching
Aerobic workouts, 166. *See also* Cross-training
Aging, 91, <u>100</u>
AIS, 70, 149. *See also* Rope stretching
Alcohol, avoiding, <u>89</u>
Altitude training, **54**, 55
Arm carriage and running form, 17

B

Back position and running form, 17
Barefoot running, <u>22</u>
Bicycling, 170
Body, listening to, <u>49</u>
Body positioning and running form, <u>18</u>
Boots, compression, 185
Boston Marathon (2014), ix, 9–10
Breakfast, 89–90
Breathing and stretching, 140

C

Cadence, <u>15</u>, 54
Caffeine, <u>88</u>
Calories burned by running, 91
Carbohydrates, 87
Challenging but realistic goals, 4–5
Chaurushiya, Suresh, **169**
Cheruiyot, Robert K., 10
Choices and goals, <u>8</u>, 93
Circulatory system stimulation machine, 188
Coffee, <u>88</u>
Commitment, x, 2, 7, 9, 47
Compex electrostimulation machine, 186, 188
Compression clothing, 185
Consistency, 2, 44–45, 47

Cooldowns, <u>52</u>, <u>185</u>
Cross-training
  bicycling, 170
  cadence and, increasing, <u>15</u>
  cycling, 170
  defining, 167
  Dos and Don'ts, <u>175</u>
  ElliptiGO, 166, **167**, 170–71, 173
  when healthy, 168–69
  when injured, 168, **169**, 171–74, 173
  integrating with running, 170–71
  intensity of, 171
  selecting, 170
  when traveling, **166**
  water running, 173
Cycling, 170

D

Delayed start of race, dealing with, <u>71</u>
Desserts, 90, <u>90</u>
Diet
  alcohol and, avoiding, <u>89</u>
  balanced, 87
  breakfast, 89–90
  caffeine and, <u>89</u>
  carbohydrates in, 87
  desserts, 90, <u>90</u>
  dietary fat in, 88
  dinner, 90
  Dos and Don'ts, <u>95</u>
  fast food in, avoiding, <u>87</u>
  foods to avoid as runner, <u>89</u>
  fruits in, <u>90</u>
  grains in, <u>89</u>, 90–91
  high-fiber foods in, <u>89</u>
  lunch, 90
  marathon and, running, 74–77
  meat in, 87–88
  post-workout, 182–83
  principles of good running, 86–98
  protein in, 87–88
  racing and, 74–77
  recovery and, 182–83
  seafood in, 87
  snacks, 90

  spicy foods in, <u>89</u>
  supplements and, <u>91</u>
  typical day's, 88–91
  vegetables in, 88
  vegetarian, <u>86</u>
Dietary fat, 88
Dinner, 90
Dos and Don'ts
  cross-training, <u>175</u>
  diet, <u>95</u>
  mental training, <u>11</u>
  racing, <u>83</u>
  recovery, <u>188</u>
  running form, <u>23</u>
  strength training, <u>102</u>
  stretching, <u>141</u>
  training, <u>57</u>
Double training, <u>45</u>
Drinking. *See* Hydration; *specific drink*
Dropping out of race, decision to, <u>78</u>
Drummond, Jon, 71
Dynamic stretching, <u>71</u>. *See also* Stretching

E

Electrolyte drinks, 70, <u>71</u>, 76, <u>76</u>
Electrostimulation machine, 186, 188
ElliptiGo, <u>45</u>, 166, **167**, 170–71, 173
Epsom salt bath, 184
Eritrean bread, <u>89</u>

F

Fanny packs, <u>17</u>
Fartleks, <u>15</u>, 55
Fast food, avoiding, <u>87</u>
Fatigue, 42
Feet
  barefoot running and, <u>22</u>
  pre-race strategies for, 70
  running form and, 16–17
  shoes and, 21–23